HOW TO LIVE & WORK IN SAUDI ARABIA

In this Series

LIVE & WORK IN
SAUDI ARABIA

A Handbook for Short and Long Stay Visitors

J. McGregor & M. Nydell

Special Consultant
Alison Lanier

How To Books

British Library Cataloguing-in-Publication Data
McGregor, Joy
How to live and work in Saudi Arabia.
—(How to books)
I. Title II. Nydell, Margaret III. Series
915.3804

ISBN 0-85703-007-9

Consultant Editor: Alison Lanier

This fully revised and updated edition first published in the UK in 1991 by
How To Books Ltd, Plymbridge House,
Estover Road, Plymouth PL6 7PZ, United Kingdom.
Tel: Plymouth (0752) 705251. Fax: (0752) 695699. Telex: 45635.

Typeset by Kestrel Data, Exeter
Printed and bound in Great Britain by
Dotesios Ltd, Trowbridge, Wiltshire.

Contents

Preface

Saudi Arabia covers an area the size of Western Europe. Many imagine it as a vast trackless desert; in fact it is a complex land of cities and universities, nomads and oases, huge farms, skyscrapers and oilfields. In the wake of the Gulf war it continues to offer well-paid jobs for a whole range of expatriates from petroleum engineers to construction workers, and accountants to doctors, nurses and teachers.

The book covers essential practical topics such as entry requirements, transport, money matters, housing, schools and insurance, plus vital pointers to Saudi Arabian values, customs, business practices and etiquette, providing a complete resource whether you are planning a stay of three months or three years.

The book also includes a variety of reference information such as further reading, a guide to average temperatures in different parts of Saudi Arabia throughout the year, a list of recommended supplies to take with you, and a guide to useful contacts in everything from official and cultural bodies to banks, business and legal organisations.

We hope all this information will help you plan a happy and successful stay.

The publishers would like to offer their grateful thanks to Mr M. Mashuq ibn Ally, Director of the Centre for Islamic Studies, St David's University College, University of Wales, who was kind enough to check the manuscript and make some very valuable comments and suggestions.

1
An Overview

The ultramodern and the ancient greet the newcomer in Saudi Arabia. In Jiddah and Riyadh (and soon in the Eastern Province) one arrives at superb modern airports. Motorways connect the airports with the cities, where modern glass and steel high-rise buildings flank boulevards choked with traffic. Gone are huge flares above the eastern oilfields, the gas now tapped off and shipped overseas. Gone too are most of the shuttered houses of Jiddah and many of the mud buildings of the Nejd. The desert, it seems, has been tamed.

The Fourth Five-Year Plan, which is well under way, has concentrated on building the country's infrastructure: roads, hospitals, airports, communications systems and schools. School enrolment at all levels has increased more than fourfold in fifteen years. There are now 18,630 miles (30,000 kilometres) of paved roads, many of which are engineering marvels like the Mecca to Taif highway with 174 twisting mountain curved in 54 miles. Nearly 28,000 miles (45,000 kilometres) of farm roads now link dozens of villages and remote areas. The country's ports process more than 50 million tons of freight per year, and the three main airports handle 24 million passengers per year. New industrial parks are under construction all over the country on the theory that development should reach beyond urban centres (for more information about the Five-year Plan, see page 31).

This country of superhighways, jets and Italian fashions still hears, five times a day, the call to prayer from the delicate minarets of ancient and modern mosques. Nowadays the **muezzins** do not climb the rickety stairs to the top of the minaret but call the faithful to prayer over a microphone or with a recorded message. The glass and concrete skyscrapers are surrounded by open-fronted shops where copper, brass, and carpets are sold, as they have been for

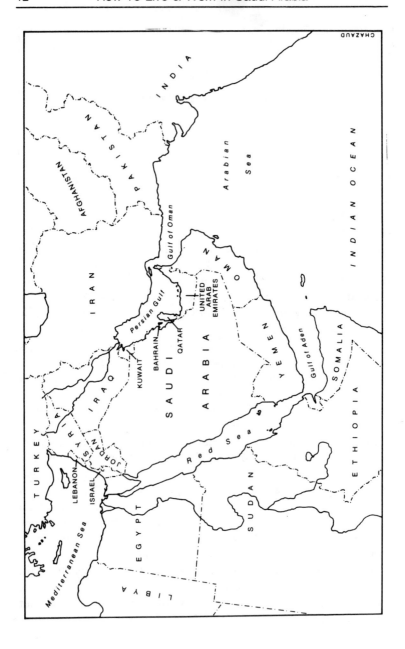

hundreds of years, by merchants puffing water-pipes (hookahs) and sitting cross-legged on the floor. Camels do not saunter down city streets as they once did: they are now in racing stables or far away in the desert beside the long black tents of the Bedouin.

The Saudis place a high value on preserving their culture and traditions. They are restoring old buildings and retaining wind towers, not because they are needed for office space or air-conditioning but because they are part of the local scene. They intend to maintain their identity as a people, a nation and the Keeper of the Faith. They are unhappy with encroaching foreign moral and cultural attitudes that threaten their beliefs even though they actively seek infusions of foreign technology to launch them into the twenty-first century. They are determined to use this new knowledge without diluting the old faith and treasured traditions.

THE COUNTRY

Saudi Arabia, often called simply 'the Kingdom', occupies four-fifths of the Arabian Peninsula, covering roughly 800,000 square miles (about the area of the United States east of the Mississippi or all of Western Europe). In our mind's eye we see a vast, trackless 'Lawrence of Arabia' desert, a land of wide open spaces and barren mountains. Saudi Arabia is that, but it is also much more: a land of new roads, villages and towns; huge farms irrigated by giant pivots; ancient oases, antiquities and nomads; cities and universities; oil wells and industry. It is a complex land which can no longer be labelled undeveloped.

The major cities on the west coast are Jiddah and Taif, as well as the holy cities of Mecca and Medina, forbidden to non-Muslims. Riyadh, the Capital, is near the centre of the country. The major cities in the oil-rich Eastern Province are Dhahran, Dammam and Al Khobar (see chapter 10 for descriptions).

The villages of Arabia are fascinating. Not long ago most were tightly packed clusters of buildings surrounded by a mud wall (for protection against raiders), small fields and date groves. Now the old village has been abandoned and given over to the goats and sheep. Nearby is a new village of concrete villas, each walled for privacy, with new schools, mosques and market-places. With the advent of deep wells and pumping systems, orchards, fields, and pasture extend around many villages.

Regions
Popular belief has it that Arabia is one giant sand-pit. In fact it is
no such thing. Wide plains, rugged mountains with wild river
valleys, and volcanic areas make up two-thirds of the country. The
other third comprises the incredible sand dunes of the deserts in
the north and south. The Arabian Peninsula, known as the Arabian
shelf, is a separate tectonic plate formed by volcanic activity and
sedimentation. Eons ago the Arabian plate broke free from the
African continent, forming the Red Sea in between. The western
edge of the plate was slowly tilted up several degrees onto its side,
which accounts for the many escarpments running north and south
in various parts of the peninsula. The two most spectacular of these
are the Hijaz Mountains in the Western Province and the Tuwaiq
Escarpment in the Nejd or Central District.

The Western Region
The Tihama Plain extends along the coast from Jiddah past Jizan
and on into Yemen. In spring the plain is green with grass and
provides grazing for the nomads' flocks. **Wadis** (huge dry river-
beds) occasionally channel monstrous flash floods out onto the
plains. In the south, around Jizan, farming continues as it always
has. Here some of the people live in round, thatched huts, telling
of their African heritage of long ago. Animals are still used for
transportation, to turn millstones and to draw water. Malarial
swamps in the south are still the cause of illness and misery. Few
foreigners come to these parts, and the area remains relatively
unchanged by the oil wealth.

All along the coast are the beautiful coral reefs of the Red Sea.
In spaces the roofs are within wading distance of the shore; in other
areas one needs a boat to reach them. From the air the coral is
clearly visible in the crystal blue sea.

Hijaz and Asir
Rising from the flat Tihama Plain bordering the Red Sea, the Hijaz
and Asir Mountains soar to 11,000 feet (3,500 metres). Blessed
with relatively abundant rainfall, these mountains are heavily
populated and intensively farmed. All along the mountain chain,
numerous tiny villages, protected by craggy peaks and cliffs, nestle
amid green, tree-shaded fields. The abundant wildlife includes
wolves, ibex, baboons, and the rarely seen caracel, a type of bobcat.
Butterflies and birds, hedgehogs and hyraxes, beetles, centipedes,

snakes, scorpions and foxes all live in the mountains as well as in
the plains and sand dunes.

The western side of the Asir is a rock wall dropping thousands
of feet to the Tihama Plain. Between Jiddah and Jizan in the south,
the Italians, master road-builders, have cut three highways down
the cliffs. One of these, the Sha'ar descent from Abha to Jizan,
drops from 6,600 feet (2,000 metres) to 4,000 feet (1,219 metres)
in 9 miles (14.5 kilometres)—a breathtaking ride.

Northern Hijaz

On the gentle eastern slopes of this range and north of Medina is
one of the largest areas of intense volcanic activity anywhere in the
world. Enormous lava beds have been formed by lava flows. The
last flow occurred in A.D. 1300 and stopped just short of the holy
city of Medina. It is a rugged region with few roads and fewer
villages.

About 200 miles (300 kilometres) north of Medina lies Madain
Salih, a lovely region of red sandstone. It is from here that the red
sands of the Nafud Desert in the north and the Dahna Sands of
the Nejd originate. Timeless winds eat at the rock and blow the
grains of sand on their journey, which eventually ends in the Rub
al Khali (the Empty Quarter), the great desert of the south.

Deserts

The red Dahna Sands are two strips of dunes crossing the plains,
connecting the Nafud in the north and the Empty Quarter in the
south. The colour of the sand changes slowly from red in the north
to pale peach in the Empty Quarter, far to the south.

The Empty Quarter, about the size of Texas, is 250,000 square
miles (647,250 square kilometres) of old dry lake-beds and sand
dunes, some as high as 700 feet, running side by side from the
north-east to the south-west. So stable that they never move, the
dunes all have names and are well known by the local Bedouin,
who can tell you exactly which dunes are safe to drive over and
which are not. Between the dunes lie the ancient lake-beds of
Arabia which tell of the days of plentiful game in an idyllic
savannah setting. Millions of prehistoric artefacts litter the Empty
Quarter: arrowheads, grinding-stones, and sometimes even pieces
of quartzite jewellery. In the eastern part of the Empty Quarter lie
the great star-shaped dunes and further east again are deadly
quicksands which can swallow up herds of sheep, men on camels

and oil exploration trucks. To probe further in the never-ending search for oil, ARAMCO lay pontoon bridges across these quick-sands to carry their equipment deep into the desert.

The Central District
The Nejd, or Central District, is composed of gravel plains dotted with alfalfa and barley farms; the granite hills of Quwayiah at the eastern edge of the Precambrian shield rock, which makes up most of the western half of the Arabian Peninsula; and the Tuwaiq Escarpment. The sandstone and limestone cliffs of the Tuwaiq run some 600 miles (900 kilometres) through the centre of the country. Towering from 1,000 to 1,500 feet along most of its length, the sheer, daunting walls of the escarpment resemble an immense fortress protecting the capital of Riyadh. Here, the box canyons and wadis of the Tuwaiq hide beautiful springs with wild date and fig trees, limestone water-holes and huge fossil beds.

North Central District
In the large agricultural areas of the north, around Buraydah and Hail, air-conditioned chicken farms and fields of barley, wheat and alfalfa produce more eggs, meat and grain than the Saudis can consume.

The Eastern Province
Under the white sand of the Eastern Province lie the great lakes of oil and gas. On the surface are the huge, ancient oases of Qatif, Haradh and Hofuf. Another less well-known treasure of the Eastern Province is its antiquities, attesting to the area's rich history. There is evidence of trade with Mesopotamia 5,000 years ago at the site of the modern cities of Dhahran, Dammam and Al Khobar. The ruined city of Thaj predates Islam by thousands of years.

Desert climate
Though temperatures in the interior can rise to about 120 degrees Fahrenheit (48.9°C) in the summer, winters can be quite cool. January temperatures in Riyadh average in the 60s but can drop to freezing at night. Snowfall in the Asir is rare but not unheard of. Cold mists and rain are the norm in the mountains during the winter months, as are thunderstorms in the summer. The coastal regions are hot and humid in the summer, cool and pleasant in the winter.

Annual rainfall may total only two to seven inches outside the
Asir. Jiddah averages only 2.5 inches; Riyadh and Dammam, about
3 inches. This may not sound like much, but often these few inches
fall in a matter of minutes, creating havoc and devastation. The
government has built holding dams in many of the wadis to prevent
flood damage and to allow the precious water to soak into the
aquifer.

Some foreigners find it difficult to adjust to a land with no rivers
or large lakes. The wadis may overflow during torrential rains, but
few flow year-round. A perennial stream now flows south of
Riyadh, carrying the treated effluent from the city. The water runs
into the lakes at Mansouriyah and finally into the sink near Al
Kharj, where it adds to the ground-water. There is also a perennial
stream in Wadi Turbah on the eastern slope of the Asir.

Less than 15 per cent of this large country is suitable for farming
without irrigation. (It is no wonder that desalinisation is such a
priority in Saudi Arabia.) The highlands of the Asir are the most
suitable for farming, having as much as 15 inches of rain per year
from the monsoons. Near Muhail a young farmer proudly related
that his family farmed without well water, that they relied entirely
on rain and their ingenious system of holding dikes and channels.

In some areas sand is a never-ending problem. In the Empty
Quarter and wherever there are dunes, sand blows across roads,
covers railway tracks and encroaches on oases. The oil companies
wage an endless war against it, and it can be a trial to the family
gardener. Where the motorways cross dunes, the sand is sprayed
with oil or asphalt to keep it stable. Yet dust is an even greater
challenge throughout the country. When the wind blows, dust sifts
into homes through every chink and crack. A major cleaning is
required after a **shammal**, with fierce north-westerly wind which
blows across the land in spring and autumn.

THE PEOPLE

Herding nomads; village farmers; sophisticated, modern and often
highly educated city dwellers and suburbanites—all are Saudis and
all are united by one binding element, the fervour of their religion.
Whether Bedouin or company executive, man or woman, the Saudi
prays five times a day and takes Islam very seriously.

Up-to-date census information is difficult to obtain; the estimated population in 1986 was 8.4 million, with an annual growth

rate of about 3 per sent. Urbanisation is encouraged by the government: in 1988, about two-thirds of the population lived in urban areas, compared with only about half twenty years ago. Raising the standard of living of both urban and rural Saudis is a high government priority. Wages have gone up (as has the rate of inflation), and food, housing, electricity and water are all heavily subsidised to help raise the overall standard of living.

The Bedouins

The nomadic Bedouins, who comprised more than half of the population until mid-century, had declined to less than 10 per cent of the population by 1980. The chief means of livelihood for these desert dwellers used to be raiding towns and caravans, trading at oases, and raising and selling animals for meat, then buying dates and vegetables in return. Their chief means of transportation across the desert used to be the camel. Today, however, a Toyota or Chevrolet is often parked next to the tent instead of the proverbial camel. These desert people are now urbanising with great speed and becoming workers in new industrial centres. They seem to welcome the change in lifestyle: the women are delighted to move from mud houses or tents into shiny new villas with running water and privacy behind walls, and many of the young tribesmen graduate from their local school and then move immediately into training for computer operation, satellite communication, or some other twentieth-century skill.

One needs to understand and respect these hardy, dignified and self-reliant people. Their knowledge of their environment is so highly trusted that they have long been called 'desert detectives'. Just as fingerprints are accepted evidence in US courts, a Bedouin's word as to a man's weight and size, deduced from footsteps in the desert sand, is taken as evidence in Saudi courts, as is his word regarding when the footprints were made. Bedouins can trace a lost man or animal—or jeep—with incredible speed and have always been a keen, astute, alert people.

The urban family

As in all parts of the world, the shift from rural to urban living is affecting family life. The traditional extended family is rapidly being replaced by urban nuclear households (father, mother and their immediate children) for those who can afford separate housing. Father-son relationships, however, remain very strong.

Most sons visit their fathers daily and live close by. Women are still cloistered within the confines of the home and are covered in public. Nevertheless, the foreigner will encounter many women who, under their coverings, are as modern and sophisticated as women anywhere in the world.

Education is now compulsory for boys and girls through primary and secondary school, and it is free and available to everyone through graduate level at the various universities. Only rarely now does the government pay for young men to study overseas and never for young women.

Until recently, life was harsh in Saudi Arabia. The average lifespan of Saudis has always been short because of desert conditions. Saudis, on the whole, are an extremely young people: more than half are under the age of twenty. Although the top leadership is not young, many in responsible positions are. Young men in their thirties head agencies with budgets in the billions. Many of the ministers are in their forties, and some of these have held high positions for eight to fifteen years.

Foreign workers
Saudi Arabia depends heavily on its estimated two million foreign workers. More than half of the foreign work-force is unskilled or semiskilled and performs nearly all manual and heavy work. These workers come from Yemen, Egypt, the Indian subcontinent, Sri Lanka and Korea. The veritable army of technicians, managers, advisers and businessmen is composed of Americans, British, Canadians, Germans, Japanese, Dutch and Koreans, most of whom work in the oil industry or on development projects. Foreign workers comprise about 25 per cent of the total population and were about 53 per cent of the total labour force in 1980 (labour statistics are variable and are tentative at best).

The demand for foreign unskilled and semiskilled labour stems partly from Saudi culture, which grants manual labour a very low status. Everyone wants to start at the top, and almost all, especially those with some education, will expect white-collar work in an office regardless of whether or not they are appropriately trained for it. A second reason for needing foreign manual labour is the great emphasis in the Saudi educational system on producing the maximum number of highly trained people to meet their immense requirements for skilled technicians and managers. Traditional education, which was geared to scholars, religious leaders and judges, was no longer adequate. During the 1940s and 1950s, the complete restructuring of the educational system reflected the Saudi awareness of its need for technical and managerial skills for the rapidly changing economy. Large numbers of foreign teachers were brought in to teach new business and technical subjects. In 1980, of the 30,000 employees of ARAMCO, 22,000 were Saudis. Over 45 per cent of the management and supervisory positions were occupied by Saudis. In 1984 the first Saudi was named president of the company.

In addition to the large number of legal foreigners in the work-force, there has been a large floating population of illegal or casual workers. Recently, the government has cracked down on these workers but has offered amnesty to those who come forward to be registered. Those who have stayed still provide service as handymen, car-washers, servants and the like. In Riyadh there is an area in Natha where these casual labourers still hire out by the day to do odd jobs.

Working women
In view of the pressing shortage of both skilled and unskilled Saudi workers, current political and religious leaders are facing a choice between what they believe to be two evils: to continue to import foreign workers, with all the inherent problems and social changes; or to adopt a more liberal policy on the employment of Saudi women. Theoretically, the employment of women has always been deplored although it has been tolerated at times because of labour shortages.

In the face of increasing traditionalism in the Gulf region in general, the government has been trying to appease Muslim conservatives at home by enforcing traditional restrictive laws—including those involving women—with increasing firmness. At the same time, officials at the Ministry of Planning are debating how women can be given a larger role in the economy without violating Islamic law. Beginning in the 1980s the government has tried to identify 'women's jobs', and Saudi women are now active in the fields of social welfare, girls' education, and health (pharmacy, dentistry, and medicine). Around 5,000 Saudi nurses are female, but nursing is still not considered a suitable career for young women.

In 1980 the first women's bank was opened. For women only and staffed by women, the bank was a success. There are now branches in all the major cities. Resistance to issuing women with driving licences is still strong because driving would reduce their present social insulation. This lack of mobility hampers women's employment opportunities, but the number of women entering the workplace has nevertheless increased dramatically. In 1981 about 50,000 Saudi women worked, and by the end of the Third Five-Year Plan in 1985, the number had climbed to about 120,000. Actually, Saudi women could replace foreigners in many positions were it not for the restrictions separating them from men.

THE PRESENT GOVERNMENT

The House of Saud

Arabian monarchs are no figureheads: they have legislative, executive and judicial power. There is no formal constitution; there are no political parties and no national elections. The king's authority is based on Arab tradition and on **shari'a** (Islamic law). His role is defined partly by recent history and tradition but also in large measure by the strong personalities of both Ibn Saud, who established the royal house, and the late King Faisal.

Each king is expected to be a patriarch who cares for his people, a **sheikh** (tribal leader), and a paramount **imam** (prayer/ congregation leader) who both upholds and interprets the tenets of Islam, albeit with the advice of **ulema** (religious scholars). Each is also, of course, the **malik** (king, or chief of state). The only title the present king uses is 'The Sheriff of the Two Holy Harams' (doubtless as a result of pressure from the religious traditionalists).

According to Arab tradition, the male members of a family (or of a tribe) come to a concensus in any important decision. In the House of Saud there are said to be some sixty to seventy family members who meet together to make key government decisions.

The disturbance in the Grand Mosque in Mecca in November 1979 and the rising power of conservative Islamic leaders throughout the area are leading to changes in the pattern of government. For example, more concern is being shown for the less affluent, the government is selling the holdings of some of its companies to its Saudi employees, and more subsidies are going to the desert tribes. These subsidies are responsible for a marked increase in the number of camels kept by the desert dwellers, which in turn raises individual, family and tribal prestige. Efforts are also increasing to spread the benefits of oil money through scholarships, housing, interest-free loans, medical facilities and an effective welfare system. Saudis hope these efforts will maintain the stability they have enjoyed since the advent of Ibn Saud.

Currently the leadership looks stable to outside observers, but the royal family, with its approximately five thousand princes, is worried. 'We are working to make this a leaner state, more closely attuned to Islam than it is today,' stated King Fahd before he succeeded to the throne. His statement is probably even more accurate today, given current pressure from the conservatives.

The family feels threatened from several directions: the disruption caused by the Gulf war, possible corruption from Western influences, and what they consider to be harsh anti-Arab propaganda and policies in other nations.

The government is run by the king, the crown prince and the Council of Ministers, many of whom are members of the royal family. The Council usually meets weekly, and all its decisions are supported by the entire Saud family. It contains representatives from twenty ministries in the government as well as three ministers without portfolio (not assigned to a particular ministry); it deals with the budget, international agreements, contracts, appointments of officials and employment of foreigners.

King Fahd, who became the fifth Saudi king after the death of King Khaled in 1982, has recognised the increasing pressure by the rising educated class for a greater role in government. In contrast, the ulema wish to maintain the status quo. The king has not overruled them, but he has reiterated his support for establishing a National Consultative Assembly, which, if formed, would broaden the base of consensus to include the nation's 200,000 bureaucrats and more than 100,000 professionals. The Assembly would provide a sounding-board for public opinion but would not replace the traditional governing units—the Council of Ministers and the king when he holds a **majlis**, or open court. Establishment of the Assembly has been delayed, however, in the face of opposition from the conservative members of the ruling class and the religious establishment.

The Saudi Association of Chambers of Commerce, however, does represent upper-level businessmen, industrialists and contractors. The Association 'plays an essential role in consolidating middle-class support for the royal family and consequently is believed to enjoy considerable influence over the regime. It is the only major organization in the Kingdom to elect its own officers' (Abir, 1988, p. 161).

The winds of modernisation blow more quickly through the business community in most countries than they do through the structures of government. So it is in Saudi Arabia. Many of the young princes and a growing number of bright young technocrats have returned from Princeton, Harvard Business School, Oxford, the London School of Economics and Political Science and elsewhere, and are already making their mark on the business world. Recent years have seen the introduction—by royal decree—of many important institutions, especially laws and regulations required by a modern state. These include laws dealing with employer-employee relations, customs regulations, civil service requirements, economic development, social security, an agricultural development bank, commercial transactions and foreign investment.

Basic domestic problems facing the Kingdom today appear to be as follows:

1. How well can it balance the nation's traditional, religious and cultural values against the need for a new political system built on a modern foundation?
2. How sensitive will the royal family be to the changing needs of a growing and increasingly sophisticated population?
3. How well can the nation deal with its own increasingly complex economy?

THE RELIGION OF ISLAM

Since Arabia is the birthplace and centre of Islam, the world's second largest religion, it is extremely important for outsiders to be well informed about it. With well over 650 million believers, it plays a major role in some ninety countries and is growing steadily.

The word **Islam** means 'submission to God'. Perhaps the most important of its teachings, from the point of view of an outsider, is that all people are equal before God. Believers attempt to live as well as teach this doctrine.

The Qur'an the Islamic holy book, contains a detailed code of ethics which Muslims learn in meticulous detail at an early age and by which they live their lives. It is their book of worship, their code of law and their standard for classical Arabic (the written language). In Saudi Arabia, in fact, the rules laid down in shari'a are the equivalent of the coutnry's constitution. Even administrative legislation is subject to shari'a, as are all new laws and regulations. Anyone going to Saudi Arabia, or to any Muslim country, should do some background reading on Islam, including selections from the Qur'an and a biography of the Prophet Muhammad (see Further Reading). This background is vital to any real understanding of Islamic attitudes, priorities, values and motivations. One major difference between the Islamic and Christian faiths is this: In Christianity, Christ is paramount, the Bible secondary. In Islam, the Qur'an is the word of God and the closest contact humans have with God; Muhammad was a prophet, highly respected but not worshipped for himself.

The five pillars of Islamic faith provide a practical, ever-present focus for all Muslims:

1. 'There is no God but God and Muhammad is His Prophet.' This confession of faith is the basic premise and is repeated throughout every day of a Muslim's life.
2. Prayers are to be said five times a day at certain hours (in public or in private) with outward physical expressions of piety, a practice which all Muslims share, whatever their status, age or importance.
3. *Zakat*, an income tax of 2½ per cent **must** be given to the poor.
4. **Ramadan** is to be kept as a fasting month for penitence, remembrance and purification.
5. **A Hajj** (pilgrimage to Mecca) should, if it is at all possible, be made some time during a Muslim's life.

Ramadan
The month of Ramadan, the ninth month of the Islamic year, is strictly observed in Saudi Arabia. Between dawn and sunset one does not eat, drink, smoke or have marital intercourse. When the sun sets, families break their fast and eat and drink together before sleeping and then eat and drink again before dawn the next day. The end of the month is celebrated with a three or four-day holiday, **Eid al Fitr**, (the Feast of the Breaking of the Fast). Westerners are not, of course, expected to keep the fast, but they are expected to respect and understand Ramadan. With the recent upswing of traditionalism has come strict enforcement of the observance of the fast.

Westerners should definitely avoid eating, drinking or smoking in public. Women should dress more conservatively, making sure they are very well covered when they go shopping.

Ramadan certainly slows down business. It is a good month for catching up, cleaning out files, doing research or taking a holiday. Work does go on but at a slower pace. As the month progresses, tempers may become short and people generally more irritable. The month of fasting and short nights are a strain on everyone. New business should generally wait, if possible, until Ramadan is over.

The Hajj

Two months after Ramadan is the pilgrimage to Mecca. Over a million Muslims—at least a third of them from other countries—congregate in Jiddah and travel to Mecca for the ceremonies. Great pilgrim tent cities are set up to care for the multitudes. Fleets of buses and trucks, used only at this time of year, are pressed into service for transportation. Most now make the pilgrimage by air; many others come by car, and still others by ship. There is a government ministry with the sole duty of preparing for and handling this annual influx of humanity. This ministry has built an incredible motorway system in the holy city, and its administrators have become masters at disease control. Saudi Arabia is considered a leading authority in the treatment of heatstroke. The ceremonies end with **Eid al Adha** (the Feast of the Sacrifice).

Holy cities

Both Mecca and Medina are considered holy, and non-Muslims are forbidden to enter. Muhammad was born in Mecca and his tomb is in Medina. Special bypasses on major roads keep non-Muslims away from Mecca and Medina. **Do not go beyond any warning sign**. You will be arrested immediately and will have no excuse for this infraction of an extremely important rule.

Muslim courtesies

The following suggestions should be followed at all times to show respect for Islam:

1. Do not walk in front of a Muslim who is praying.
2. Do not walk across prayer rugs
3. Show respect to those who are praying by refraining from taking

pictures, by talking softly or not at all, and by moving no more than necessary (especially avoid fast motion).

4. Never use the word Mohammedan. Use Muslim instead.

Shari'a, the foundation of Islamic Law

(This section is based on Laron Jensen, *Business America*, 30th June 1980.)

Westerners doing business in the Islamic world should be familiar with the roots of Islamic legal tradition as embodied in shari'a, considered sacred law grounded in divine revelation. In most Middle East/North African countries, shari'a either coexists alongside secular laws of Ottoman, Egyptian, French or British origin or has been relegated mainly to matters of personal and family affairs. In some countries, notably Saudi Arabia, shari'a takes precedence over all other government regulations. Briefly outlined here are aspects of shari'a relevant to Western businessmen.

Shari'a is based on four principal sources. Primary sources, accepted by major Islamic sects and schools of legal thought, include the Qur'an, containing the Word of God as given to the Prophet, and the **Sunna**, which are the sayings, acts and allowances of the Prophet as recorded by reliable authorities in the **Hadiths** (traditions). Secondary sources of shari'a include **iima**, usually defined as a historical consensus of qualified legal scholars, and **giyas**, analogical reasoning which is used for circumstances not provided for in other sources. An example of the latter is the acceptance by twentieth-century shari'a scholars of the presentation of human images on television. Acceptance of the secondary sources of shari'a varies among Islamic groups.

Shari'a legal precepts can be categorised into five areas: acts commanded, recommended, reprobated, forbidden and left legally indifferent. Shari'a mandates rules of behaviour in the areas of social conduct, family relations, inheritance and religious ritual, and defines punishments for heinous crimes including adultery, false accusation of adultery, intoxication, theft and robbery. Punishments and rules not defined by the historical sources of shari'a are left to decision by Islamic judges and/or according to contemporary government regulations. This practice has permitted an evolution of shari'a law to reflect changed social, political and economic conditions in Muslim societies.

Significant similarities between shari'a and Western law include equality before the law (no privileges to the ruler), innocence until proof of guilt, burden of proof placed on the plaintiff, sanctity of written contracts, and the existence of a system of appeal procedures.

Other aspects of shari'a relevant to the conduct of business include the following:

1. **Evidence:** Claims generally must be substantiated by two male witnesses (preferably Muslims), or one male and two females, or one male and the oath of the claimant. For adultery four male witnesses are required. Character witnesses may be required to substantiate the repute of other witnesses. Hearsay is generally not accepted as evidence. In the absence of written evidence, sworn oral evidence is sufficient. Words are accepted according to their normal meaning.

2. **Precedent:** While judges are bound to respect the traditional sources of shari'a, a particular ruling of a judge is not binding on other judges or on himself in a diffrent case.

3. **Lending:** The giving or taking of interest is forbidden by shari'a. However, Islamic law permits management or service fees, discounting, loans having the appearance of a sale (in which the borrower sells to the lender with an agreement to repurchase later at a higher price), lending of property to another to invest with profits to be shared in proportions previously agreed upon (risks, however, remaining with the lender), and sharing in business risks (profits or losses).

4. **Secured transactions:** The pledging of personal property is allowed. The pledgee assumes possession of the collateral but generally must apply to the courts to sell it.

5. **Standards of damages:** These are quite simple and modest under shari'a: for property damage, actual cost of repair or replacement; for unintentional death, a fixed sum ($30,000 for Muslim males and $15,000 for Muslim females; in the case of non-Muslims, half the stated amount). Age is not a consideration. The loss of 'opportunity cost' of money is not compensated under shari'a. A recent change in the law states that any damage caused by animals loose on the highway is the responsibility of the animal's owner, not the person whose vehicle hit the beast. Needless to say, it is very difficult to collect any compensation in these cases. Foreigners are advised to carry adequate insurance on personal vehicles.

6. **Force majeure:** Acts of God are accepted as defence for non-performance of a contract. In typical shari'a court proceedings, neither lawyers nor formal written proceedings are required. In criminal cases a defendant cannot delegate his defence to a lawyer. The Islamic **qadi** (judge) seeks the truth by questioning all parties to a dispute, including witnesses. Judges may not use their own knowledge of a fact as the basis for a decision. If a judge is changed during a proceeding, the new judge should rehear the entire case. Judges are encouraged to foster compromise between disputants rather than adjudicate a claim, but they will do the latter when mediation fails. Cases should be speedily heard in a court closest to the defendant's home, regardless of where a contract is executed. Civil (private right) and criminal (public right) aspects of a case can be treated together in the same trial. An example of a case involving both aspects would be a traffic accident in which there is a private right to recover damages to property or person and a public right to punish a violation of the vehicle regulations. Sentences are imposed by the judge and carried out by a representative of the government, for example, the provincial governor in Saudi Arabia.

In Saudi Arabia, which exemplifies the shari'a court system, there are four levels of shari'a courts, supplemented by nearly a dozen administrative tribunals responsible for specific regulations of a ministry or other agency of government. Examples of the latter include the Committee for Settlement of Commercial Disputes, the Committee for Settlement of Labour Disputes, and the Grievance Board.

The shari'a courts include **general courts** (most common), with one or more judges having responsibility for personal, family, civil and criminal matters; **limited courts**, with one judge, generally handling smaller cases involving civil or criminal matters; and two appeals courts. The **Court of Appeals**, with five or more judges, is generally the highest shari'a appeals court. However, it has no jurisdiction over the other administrative tribunals or disputes between a lower shari'a court and another tribunal. The **Supreme Judicial Council**, the fourth shari'a court, handles matters referred to it by the king, considers appeals from other courts, and reviews lower court sentences involving death or mutilation.

In practice, civil claims in Saudi Arabia can also be referred to the **amir** (governor) of a province, who can use his good offices to settle complaints; failing this, the amir will refer claims to a shari'a court. Commercial disputes can be arbitrated by chambers of commerce and industry in key cities. Finally, the **Grievance Board**, not a shari'a court but whose members include both shari'a and secular-trained legal counsellors, draws its authority from the king's power to administer justice and redress grievances by individuals who allege wrongdoing by the government. The Grievance Board has jurisdiction over any complaint submitted to it, principally involving complaints against government agencies and their administrative regulations.

Islam and westernisation

Although Westerners frequently use the words interchangeably, *westernising* and *modernising* are two quite different ideas. Most of the world is eager to modernise; most of it does **not** want to westernise. Leadership in Saudi Arabia has become increasingly cautious in this regard as jolting events have strengthened its natural conservatism and as foreigners have flooded its cities.

No uprising like that in Iran is expected; nor is it likely that Saudi Arabia will be subject to the kind of internal turmoil that has afflicted other Arab countries. The reasons are numerous:

1. In Saudi Arabia the ruling family does not flaunt its wealth.
2. No working class solidarity exists, nor is there a generation of Saudi students harbouring discontent in foreign cities and reflecting it to the nations' youth at home.
3. The small but growing business middle class is too busy making money to be actively critical.
4. Politics are not talked about openly as they are in Cairo or most Western cities.
5. Above all, a strict form of Islam permeates the Saudi society from top to bottom.

Further more, as we have noted above, the royal family learned from observing the revolution in Iran. For example, because of complaints in Iran against the concentration of spending in the cities while the outlying areas were neglected, the Saudis are paying increased attention to agriculture and the quality of life in rural communities.

We mentioned the disturbance in the Grand Mosque in Mecca

in 1979. The government's successful management of the outburst attested to its strength but also showed its dependence on the goodwill of traditional, conservative religious leaders. As a result, security has also been stepped up in all holy areas.

King Fahd and Crown Prince Abdullah have prudently included the ulema in their decision-making. The royal family is widespread and attuned to popular traditionalist feelings, giving in to many of their demands in order to strengthen domestic support. These Saudi traditionalists are deeply upset (as Muslim traditionalists are in much of the Middle East) not only by the rapid infusions of Western technology they are experiencing, but by the influx of Western ideas and customs as well. They also worry about the exploitation of their vast, but finite, oil resources. Security is tight throughout the country, and foreigners have learned to keep a low profile.

The royal family and the nation's religious leaders are adamant that progress not be allowed to erode the religious foundations of the nation. Therefore, side by side with the ultramodern factories and complex computerised systems are the strict Islamic values: no alcohol; the closing of shops at prayer times; segregation of women from men at work and in school; relegation of foreigners to their own compounds, where they can exert minimum influence on Saudi society; and media that are carefully controlled and saturated with religious messages.

THE ECONOMY

In roughly fifty years Saudi Arabia has changed from a desert backwater with a simple nomadic system of trade and barter to a modern, complex and extremely wealthy society. In that short time, the country has risen to the forefront of many international financial debates and taken a major role in the world's monetary system. This incredible development was, of course, the result of the discovery of oil in 1938. Until 1970 ARAMCO (a subsidiary of Standard Oil of New Jersey, Standard Oil of California, Texaco, and Mobil) owned the rights to most of this oil and controlled its production, paying royalties to the Saudi government. Now, though ARAMCO continues to operate the company, the Saudi government fully owns these rights and production facilities.

Saudi Arabia sits atop one-quarter of the world's known oil resources: its reserves are greater than those of the United States and USSR. combined. In 1981 it was estimated that at the present rate of extraction, the oil would last forty-five years, but Saudi Arabia lowered its rate in 1983, thereby extending the life of its wells. Furthermore, many experts expect discoveries of even more oilfields.

The Fourth Five Year Plan

Saudi Arabia has planned and executed four ambitious and highly successful five-year plans, beginning with the first in 1970. The general goals of the plans include:

● diversifying the economy to lessen dependence on oil;
● increasing production of goods for local consumption;
● improving technology, transportation, and communications; and
● upgrading education to decrease gradually dependence on foreign workers.

Each plan has been more ambitious than the last in terms of promoting agriculture, industry, electrification, education and training, and health care.

The Fourth Five-Year Plan was launched in March 1985 and was budgeted at 1,000 billion Saudi riyal (SR) (approximately $US277 billion). Half of this amount was devoted to human resources development, health and social services, transportation and communications, and housing (the remaining half was used for defence, education, the Hajj and foreign aid). Construction projects have included schools in large numbers, highways, airports, harbour and port facilities, hospitals, a new telephone system, and low-cost housing.

The Plan also adopted a 'programme approach' in planning government expenditures, emphasising whole programmes rather than individual projects. For example, the government has set up a royal commission for the planning and construction of the new industrial cities of Jubail and Yanbu, which are largely completed. The population of Jubail is projected at 300,000 by the year 2000 and the population of Yanbu at about 150,000. The price tag for Jubail is 45 billion dollars, making it the world's largest construction site during the 1970s and 1980s. Located there are petroleum refineries, petrochemical plants and related industries. In both cities the industrial zone accommodates the primary (refining,) petroleum industries run by Petromin (General Petroleum and Minerals Organisation) and SABIC (Saudi Arabian Basic Industrial Corporation). In Jubail 120 potential secondary industries have been identified, including those which manufacture plastics, copper, steel and aluminium products. Unlike the primary industries, these are to be established by private firms. New industrial cities are also planned for Medina, the Asir, Mecca, Hail, Tabuk, Jizan and Najran. Major firms from the United States, the United Kingdom, Europe and Japan are participating in the development of these cities under joint venture agreements.

The Saudi government continues to encourage increased participation in joint ventures on the part of middle-sized firms. To this end it is contracting work in smaller segments so that more firms, both foreign and Saudi, can become involved. The government also supports the trend toward giving a larger economic role to the private sector, which contributed one-third of the GNP in 1985, compared with 13 per cent in 1975.

Fast-growing sectors of the economy include not only heavy and light industries but also housing, food products, and services. Massive importation will continue, however, for many years, with foreign firms competing for a large, wide-open market. Education and vocational training were strongly emphasised in the Fourth Plan and received 12.5 per cent of the budget. By the end of the five years, the number of male and female students at the elementary level have increased significantly, with similar increases at higher levels. Saudi Arabia's eight universities have sixteen campuses country-wide, and more universities, community colleges and vocational institutes are planned.

2
Before Leaving

ENTRY PAPERS AND REQUIREMENTS

Passport

You will, of course, need a passport to go to Saudi Arabia. In addition to the photos you need for the passport, you may want to take a supply of passport pictures (about six to ten) with you, although recent reports from expatriates indicate they are not often needed. Although it is not required, some businessmen advise taking photocopies of any professional certificates, including university degrees, as these can sometimes be helpful.

Your employer will ask for your passport on arrival, keep it in a safe during your stay, and return it when you depart. The rationale for this practice is that the company assumes complete responsibility for you while you are in the Kingdom. There do seem to be some inconsistencies in this practice, however, and occasionally individuals are permitted to keep their passports when they are on a short visit.

Be aware that valid passports are in great demand all over the world among terrorists, narcotics dealers, guerrillas and others. Prices offered for them by the underworld are often in the thousands of dollars. Therefore, the world's finest pickpockets haunt major airports. While you are in transit, guard your passport carefully; never put it down even for a minute in a terminal (or anywhere else, for that matter); do not let it show in your pocket or attaché case. A zippered or inside pocket is the best hiding-place.

No passport with an Israeli entry stamp is valid in Saudi Arabia, and entry is difficult (though not impossible) for Jews.

Visas

In addition to a passport, everyone going to Saudi Arabia will need a visa. To obtain your visa, you will need a current passport and a completed visa application with a black-and-white photo, plus documents or procedures required for specific visas listed below. The process will take from one to three weeks. When applying by mail, enclose a stamped, self-addressed envelope. Visa applications and information can be obtained from the visa section at any Saudi embassy in the world.

The visa requirements sheet includes a question about religion. This is not an optional query: an answer is mandatory. In fact, do not ever leave blank on any Saudi form the line that asks for your religious affiliation. Saudis have strong negative feelings about agnostics and atheists.

Tourist visa

No tourist visas are issued to Saudi Arabia at the present time.

Business visa

Business visas are usually initiated in Saudi Arabia. The applicant's firm or agent in Saudi Arabia must apply on his behalf to the Ministry of Foreign Affairs. If the application is approved., Saudi Arabian authorities will instruct their embassy to issue the required visa. If your Saudi sponsor is not in Saudi Arabia at the time you apply, you must attach to the application a letter from your firm, which states the purpose and length of your visit and the firm's assumption of full financial responsibility for any action taken or contracts made during your visit. It is extremely difficult for single women to obtain these visas or even to enter the country.

We recommend that you request a multiple exit/re-entry visa: it will save a lot of time if you plan to travel in and out of the country.

Business visa for short visit

A business visit visa is valid for only one trip to Saudi Arabia and is normally good for thirty days but may be extended to three months, depending on the nature of the visit. Applicants for a business visit visa must present a letter from their home company and from the Saudi Arabian company sponsoring them, stating the purpose of their visit. In some cases Saudi Arabian embassy and consular offices are permitted to grant short-visit visas to foreign businessmen without referral to the Ministry of Foreign Affairs (when the applicant is with a large corporation already established in Saudi Arabia, for example), but the normal procedure is to go through the ministry.

The procedure for obtaining a visa for a short business visit is as follows:

1. Obtain and fill out the white visa application form and attach one photo.
2. Submit your passport (must be valid for at least three months from the date of the visa request).
3. Attach the letters of support referred to above.
4. Pay the required fee with a money order or certified cheque made out to 'Saudi Consulate General' (no personal cheques are accepted).
5. Post the application and other documents to the embassy, enclosing a stamped, self-addressed envelope.
6. Foreign-born applicants must also attach a copy of their immigration papers.

Employment block visa
This visa is used only by major employers such as ARAMCO, large hospitals, hotels and construction firms that bring in hundreds of workers. Those applying for a visa which is one of an employment block group must supply all of the items listed above and in addition must

1. complete a biographical data form (blue) and submit it in English and Arabic;
2. submit a passport good for six months from the date of application;
3. attach a copy of university degrees;
4. attach a copy of the signed contract;
5. ensure that the block visa number from the sponsoring company in Saudi Arabia is included in the letter; and
6. attach a Letter of No Objection if the applicant has previously worked in Saudi Arabia.

Family visit visa
If you are working in the Kingdom without your family, family members can obtain a family visit visa. The employed spouse must submit a request of invitation to the Saudi Ministry of Foreign

affairs in Saudi Arabia, who will then wire a telex of invitation to the consulate in your country. The family member (or members) then submits a completed white visa application, a photo, a passport good for six months from the date of application, and a money order for the fee. If a wife is visiting her husband, she must supply a copy of their marriage certificate. If a child is visiting a parent, a copy of the birth certificate is required. The Saudi government now encourages all workers making more than 3,000 SR per month to bring their families with them. However, whether or not this actually happens depends on whether the employing company agrees to go to the trouble of sponsoring family members.

Exit Visas

Exit visas are required on leaving Saudi Arabia. Passports should be left with the airlines, or embassy at least a week prior to departure so that formalities can be completed. It pays to check on regulations well in advance of your departure.

Work and residence permits

Applications for work permits for foreigners are made by the employer (or sponsor) to the Ministry of the Interior and then approved by the Ministry of Labour and Social Affairs. Anyone wanting to stay longer than three months must also have a residence permit.

Your **igama** (residency permit) is issued by the Ministry of Foreign Affairs and is usually valid for two years. If you have children under fifteen, a passport-sized photo of your wife with the children is needed to register the family on your igama.

Igamas are white for Muslims and brown for non-Muslims. This document functions as an identification card and can be used for cashing cheques, in case of an accident, or at a police checkpoint. Some companies do not allow employees to carry their igama unless they go out of town. You should, however, carry a copy of the document with you at all times.

We cannot emphasise enough the importance of staying alert to the expiration dates of both your residence permits and your visas. If these documents expire, you may be in serious trouble. Since the seizure of the mosque in November 1979 the government has firmly enforced its decree to prosecute and punish aliens without residence papers. Memorise the expiration date or pencil it inside the cover of your igama. We also recommend writing down the expiration dates in a place where you glance frequently, like on a refrigerator or bulletin board.

CUSTOMS REGULATIONS

Customs regulations are strict and must be obeyed with scrupulous care. The brochure. 'Tips for Travellers to Saudi Arabia', describes import restrictions and is available from the visa section of any Saudi embassy. Instructions read as follows:

- You may not bring any alcoholic beverages with you into Saudi Arabia. It is against the law. Saudi customs inspectors are thorough. The possession of even a miniature bottle of alcohol purchased en route is a violation of the law which can subject you to a fine, possible arrest, or even deportation. Arriving in an intoxicated condition can seriously delay your clearance through immigration and customs and may result in your arrest.
- You must not carry heroin, opium, cocaine, marijuana, or any other narcotic with you without a prescription signed by your physician. Penalties for the illegal import, possession, or trafficking in narcotics in the Kingdom are severe and may involve jail sentences of up to twenty-five years.
- You may not bring in explosives, new or antique firearms, edged weapons, or pornography. Also prohibited are articles bearing the Star of David (the six-pointed star). Such items are confiscated as are other religious articles such as Bibles, crucifixes, and so on belonging to any religion other than Islam. Religious statues, carvings and the like may be either destroyed or re-exported at the owner's expense.

On one occasion people returning from vacation in Kenya had their souvenir carvings confiscated. The objects were retrieved by a Saudi expediter from their company, but it was a disconcerting experience. Such objects should probably be shipped home from the country of origin. Surprisingly, most books about Saudi Arabia, Arabs or Islam are prohibited.

Fears that foreigners may be smuggling contraband (including guns) into the country have led to strict customs inspections of all incoming shipments rather than the earlier procedure of spot-checking one shipment in five.

Currency regulations

There are no restrictions on the import or export of currency.

Pets

With the proper papers verifying immunisations, it is possible to bring dogs or cats into the Kingdom. Because of the long distance of the flight and possible refusal of entry for the pet upon arrival, however, it is best to leave your pets at home. Another deterrent to bringing a pet is that pet dogs must be kept confined or on a leash. Stray dogs are considered a nuisance and a health hazard and may be shot by the authorities. Cats must be kept in because of the risk of disease and because they cannot defend themselves against the feral cats, which are much more savage than our domesticated varieties. Also, veterinarians are difficult, though not impossible, to find. If you like pets, there are hundreds of stray cats in the Kingdom, most of which are similar to Abyssinian cats and have very interesting personalities. Or one can obtain a Saluki dog (at great expense) from the Bedouin. There are pet shops in all the major cities where one can obtain exotic birds, goldfish, or guinea pigs and hamsters. For large sums of money a person can also buy baby lions, llamas or tigers.

Importation of personal and household goods

For several years no customs duties were charged on personal items. Now, however, customs/import duties may be charged on any of the following items: radio equipment, sporting equipment, cameras, typewriters, musical instruments and tape recorders. Only limited quantities of tobacco are allowed (check with the nearest Saudi consulate). All books, periodicals, pictures, films, records or tapes may be censored for politics or pornography. Do not take in any magazines such as *Playboy* or *Esquire* that show the human form in scanty or no clothing (including art books). Most customs officials speak and read English and will quickly recognise banned books.

All household goods being sent to Saudi Arabia must be listed. the inventory should be typed double-spaced in English, and it must clearly show the contents of every container. Each item must be declared as new or old and every manufacturer's name listed as well. All new items must be declared and the bill of sale attached to the inventory. If officials find a new item among goods declared as used, they will either hold the item until you produce the bill of sale or declare the value themselves and assess duty accordingly. (At the time of writing, Sears goods, which are boycotted, are still being confiscated.)

If they do not have a correct and detailed inventory, customs officials may open and diligently inspect all shipments piece by piece—even item by item. You may end up paying overtime to the customs inspector for this 'service'. Furthermore, you cannot go to the airport to clear your household shipment through customs yourself: an Arabic-speaking broker will have to do this for you, and without a proper inventory, you will have to pay a surcharge for the broker's overtime and often for additional assisting personnel as well. Many firms provide a clearing agent to help families get their household goods through customs; some removal companies also provide that service. It is almost imperative to have Aarbic-speaking help: an individual cannot operate on his own without great difficulty—if at all—in this matter. Negotiate customs assistance with your company in Saudi Arabia *before* leaving home.

FURNISHINGS AND GOODS TO TAKE

Most companies provide furnished living accommodations for their employees, often equipped with everything from large furniture and appliances down to potato peelers. Other companies will issue a furnishing allowance once their employee arrives, and still others give a shipping allowance of several hundred pounds. Most companies provide full room and board for their single employees. It is very important to have a clear picture of your company's policies before beginning to plan what you will take.

In major cities you will be able to buy any household item you might need. You can often stock your household through garage sales held by departing expatriates. Check the bulletin boards in the supermarkets, or ask the women's organisations for dates and directions to the sales.

Appliances
Many people recommend buying large appliances on arrival since the cost of transporting them is high. Furthermore, those bought in Saudi Arabia—Japanese, German, American, or British make— have service agreements, and spare parts are more likely to be

available. Refrigerators are fairly expensive but come in all sizes. Most kitchens are set up to use propane gas in cylinders as cooking fuel, so gas stoves are needed. Many people take washing-machines. Dryers are not really necessary; the sun dries everything in about thirty minutes (you generally hang laundry on the roof). Some people prefer dryers, though, because the sun fades colours and blowing sand gets into your laundry. In general, when considering whether or not to take your own appliances, remember the harshness of the climate and the effects of sand and dust on machinery. Another consideration is electrical current, which can be problematic for imported appliances (see chapter 6 for complete information on electricity).

Furniture
You will find a large selection of furnishings available—Italian, American, French, Danish and locally made furniture. Check each item carefully before buying; not only might you find considerable breakage (customs officials can—and do—open anything coming into the country), but furnishings take a beating from the heat, dryness and dust, despite air-conditioning. Lamps are available, but they may not be to your taste.

Other suggestions
What you take with you will, of course, depend on your company's baggage or freight allowance, but we hope the following recommendations will be helpful. Keep the boycott in mind when packing. and ask at the consulate for current rulings or restrictions (see chapter 3).

1. You may want to consider taking your own kitchen and dining utensils. There is a large variety of reasonably priced dishes, glassware and crystal available in Saudi Arabia, but it takes time to find things at the **souq** (bazaar), though perhaps no longer than it will take your shipment to arrive.
2. Bed linens are available and cost about the same as in the United Kingdom, but the variety is limited. Warm woollen blankets are expensive in Saudi Arabia, but Yemeni blankets (wonderful cotton quilts) are sold in the souqs and will keep everyone warm at night.
3. If you find cupboard space too small in your new home, you can purchase extra wardrobes locally. It is usually not worth

taking up your weight allowance to bring such heavy items with you.

4. There is no need to take vacuum cleaners or any small electrical items. All small kitchen appliances, such as toasters, mixers and irons are available and reasonably priced. (If you need more convincing, read the section on electricity in chapter 6).

5. You may want to take sugar and meat thermometers. Oven thermostats vary, and you may be thankful for an oven thermometer while you figure out your new appliance.

6. Bring your own cookbooks. If you want to learn new culinary skills and recipes from other countries, there are recipe books available from several different places. Also, the women's clubs often offer cooking classes in Oriental, Arabic or French food.

7. It is a good idea to take along a small travel iron and at least one battery alarm clock to use until you can go to the souq or supermarket to obtain others to meet your needs.

8. A good set of hand tools for household repairs is a wise choice, as are tools for any kind of craft or hobby you enjoy.

9. Be sure to arrange for your subscription magazines to be sent to you. They will arrive two to three months late but will still be very welcome.

10. Windows are completely different shapes and sizes so leave draperies and curtains at home. Textiles are lovely, and good draperies and slipcovers can be made for you locally.

11. Normal pharmaceuticals are available. Cosmetics are in remarkably good supply, most of them imported from the United Kingdom and Europe. Tampax, Kleenex, soaps and hair sprays are all available.

12. Photographic film is readily available, but be sure to check expiration dates and keep unused film in the refrigerator. Printing is unreliable, so find a good developer and stick with him; most likely his prices will be fair. It would be wise to leave family albums at home; fundamentalist customs officials may consider them inappropriate and confiscate them.

13. If you bring videotapes or home movies, they will be taken and censored, and they may or may not be returned to you. It is better to build a video library once you are settled.

14. Cigarettes are available at moderate prices, as are good lighters and fuels.

15. Take books, musical instruments, and supplies for any hobbies which can keep you engrossed for long hours. This is the moment to tackle that skill you have always 'meant to learn someday', be it wood carving, playing an instrument, learning a language or painting. Take all supplies and materials that you will need. If you use your time in Saudi Arabia in a purposeful way, you will enjoy yourself far more.

16. Adult games are a wise choice. Take Monopoly, chess, backgammon, Trivial Pursuit, Pictionary, or any other games which you and your family and friends can enjoy for long periods of time together. Many families keep large jigsaw puzzles going all the time on a side table, trading them among their friends.

17. If you have children, take plenty of toys that use imagination and provide long hours of play. A huge array of toys is also available in Saudi Arabia, but they are a little more expensive than at home.

18. Take a large library of books for the children and for yourself. The Book of Knowledge or another child's encyclopaedia will help supplement the school library. Books of games, puzzles, experiments, and the like will provide young people with the extra stimulus to help them amuse themselves. Being compelled to be resourceful may turn out to be one of the best by-products of the whole experience, and parents can help to foster creativity by planning ahead. Girls often become adept at making clothes, for example, but to do so they need patterns, sewing books, and basic sewing supplies.

19. Western TV sets will not work in Saudi Arabia, but an enormous variety of five- and eight-system TVs and VCRs are available, and prices are cheaper than in the United Kingdom. All types of radios are available and inexpensive (see chapter 9 for more on radios and television).

20. Stereo components, tape recorders, reel-to-reel systems, tapes and records are in plentiful supply. Music shops often carry a huge supply of pirated music tapes, but the quality varies considerably. CDs are also available at a high price. Many music shops do not allow women to enter to buy tapes, but this rule, like many others, changes with the season and depends upon the zealousness of the religious police assigned to the area.

21. There are many companies marketing personal computers,

both recognised brands such as IBM or Apple, and 'clones' made in Taiwan or elsewhere for sale outside Europe and the United States. The brand-name machines are expensive, the clones less so. Clones, of course, cannot legally be taken into the United States. Before you buy a computer abroad, find out about import regulations in your own country. You would not want to have to abandon your computer system at the port of entry.

22. Sporting goods are available but the variety is limited, and they are also quite expensive. Bring your own equipment to the extent possible.

23. Finally, take such things as playing cards and bridge tallies, personal stationery and greeting cards, home permanents, shower curtains and hooks, typewriter ribbons and carbon paper, and any other items you personally feel are essential.

CLOTHING

As said before, most people think of Saudi Arabia as a hot desert land. Indeed, it is at most times of the year, but the weather can also be surprisingly cool. In Jiddah you will need some light, wool clothes, which you should bring with you since they are not easily obtainable locally. Cold desert winds and sandstorms blow through Riyadh and send people rushing for coats and turtlenecks. Cold-weather clothes will also be needed for holidays outside the country.

As we explain below, clothing and shoes are readily available and very stylish; fabric is lovely, and with quality tailoring you can have much of your clothing made for you. It is wise, however, to bring a good supply of clothes with you since it will take you quite some time to become acquainted with the shopping areas and *souqs* and to find a tailor to your liking. Also bring a few zippered bags to protect your nice clothing from dust and sand (these bags can also be found in the luggage souq).

Men's clothes

The order of the day for men's clothing is khaki or lightweight cotton trousers and white, short and long-sleeved cotton or cotton-blend shirts. Cotton underwear and handkerchiefs are available, but cotton socks are not. Suits should also be lightweight and cool. Bring jackets and ties for social functions. When the weather is hot (from April to September or October), men wear suit jackets only in top-level business meetings, in hotel lobbies, and sometimes in the cooler evenings. Sandals are more comfortable than shoes because of both heat and sand and are completely acceptable daytime wear except in the office. Sneakers are also widely used and are readily available in sporting goods shops at very cheap prices.

Many shops specialise in European and American men's clothing. Beautiful Italian shirts, suits and shoes are available but at a higher price than at home, and the range of sizes may be limited.

Women's clothes

Conservatism in women's dress rules at all times in the Kingdom. Within the foreign compound, you may wear what you wish, but outside you must conform to Saudi dress standards. Rebellion will only earn you a warning or a sharp flick on the legs from the cane of a religious policeman as well as harassment by males of many nationalities who will consider you morally loose and therefore fair game. In public, women should be well covered and inconspicuous. The basic rule of thumb is loose clothing, modest necklines (blouses buttoned up to the chin, turtlenecks, and so on), midcalf-length dresses or skirts, and below-the-elbow sleeves. It is also more comfortable to have your hair well covered. Heavy makeup will make you feel hot and is not appropriate. The variety within these limitations, though, is considerable. Actually, once you are used to the idea, you will find the loose and flowing clothing cool and comfortable and a welcome protection from the searing sun.

Long **thobes** (caftans) are common and very comfortable. Slacks with loose, long blouses or tunics, and long dresses are also acceptable daytime wear. Pakistani women's clothes—a long, loose tunic over matching baggy trousers—can be purchased and are most acceptable as well as being very comfortable and pretty. Saudi women are still heavily veiled and draped in black.

An added note on veils. Understanding the traditional reason behind the wearing of veils helps dispel the feeling that women who wear this ancient garment are perhaps a little inferior to the rest of us. The custom dates from pre-Islamic Persian times and was carried along the trade routes into the Arabian Peninsula. At the time of Muhammad, raiding was one of the ways nomads and villages supplemented their wealth. Governing the conduct of the raiders were some very stringent rules. Sheep, goats and camels were all fair game; crops could be destroyed and protective walls razed; also slaves could be captured and carried off. Horses, children and women, however, were not to be touched or harmed. The women of 'believers' (Muslims) were told to 'draw their veils about them that they may be recognised and left unmolested'. Wearing a veil today has essentially the same effect; veiled women are left unmolested and are treated with more respect than are those who go about with bare faces.

For evening wear, most women choose long skirts or long dresses with long sleeves. Dressy trouser suits are acceptable in the evenings in Western homes. Take several one-piece bathing suits (keep bikinis for vacations) as you will find many opportunities for swimming. Also take other sportswear, especially riding apparel if you like the sport.

US and European women's clothes are available in Saudi Arabia, but they will be a little more expensive than at home. Specialty shops, such as Wrangler jeans, Nike shoes and Benetton sweaters abound, and in the souqs you can find wonderful bargains from the Far East like sequined or beaded jackets and bags, which cost 'an arm and a leg' in the United Kingdom. Fitting rooms in women's shops are forbidden—you will have to take clothing home to try it on, and beware: if it does not fit, you may return the garments for exchange only. No refunds are allowed.

As mentioned earlier, skilled dressmakers can make stunning clothes from the beautiful fabrics imported from all over the world. Most women take advantage of this to have clothes tailor-made. If you enjoy sewing, you are fortunate. Bring your own machine if possible, but you can also find many makes in the electric souq.

Shoes
Buying shoes in Saudi Arabia is a pleasure. Gorgeous women's shoes in all styles and colours are available from Italy, Hong Kong, Thailand and South America. They are reasonably priced, but, unfortunately, are not available in large sizes. You will find no sensible shoes for work or for walking, so bring your own from home. Men's shoes range from cheap to Gucci. Regardless of what Arab counterparts wear, foreign men should not wear slipperlike shoes or sandals in the office.

Children's clothes
Many shops specialise in children's clothes, and prices are

comparable to the United Kingdom, but you will want to take plenty with you for the same reason you bring your own clothes—it will take you some time to learn your way around town. Children's clothes should be good quality, durable and perma-press. Long trousers are hot—take mostly shorts and light shirts for young children, lightweight dresses for girls. However, warm caps, scarves, sweaters, pyjamas and slippers are welcome when the winter winds blow.

Older boys wear corduroys, blue jeans or washable slacks and T- shirts or sport shirts for school; bright colours are fine. Girls wear dresses or trousers to school, but they should be as modest as their mothers.

Baby clothes are available in profusion. Bring cloth nappies if you prefer to use them or for times when disposables are temporarily unavailable. Disposable nappies can usually be found in the major cities.

Other services

Laundry and pressing services are reasonably good, and dry cleaning is now available and quite reliable. Shoe repair is set up primarily for men's shoes and is only fair in quality. Beauty shops are frowned upon and operate under cover, rather like the speak-easies of Prohibition days in the United States. Most foreign women do their own hair; appliances, perm solutions and shampoos can be purchased.

RESUMÉ OF RECOMMENDED SUPPLIES

This list does not include everything you will need. It shows articles which are either in short supply in Saudi Arabia or are not available.

1. Prescriptions—you should take at least a three-month supply to last until you find a local source of supply or can order more from home.
2. Spectacles—take extra pairs and a copy of your prescription.
3. Sunglasses—after you arrive there, you will find a local supply, but you must have a good dark pair to start with.
4. At least one alarm clock to start with; there are plenty in the souqs.

5. Shower curtains, liners, and hooks—these are available but not in great variety.
6. Bathing-suits and caps—modest one-piece suits for women and girls. You can take your bikini, but you will probably want to save it for vacations.
7. Lingerie—there are many interesting items available, but they may not be to your taste.
8. Children's and babies' clothing—again there is plenty available, but you will need time to find an outlet, look things over and compare prices.
9. Space savers for cupboard space.
10. Sports gear—add to what you bring after you find the sports shops.
11. Toiletries and cosmetics—bring any you are especially fond of. (Remember French perfume is very cheap in Saudi Arabia.)
12. Hair colour, rinse or home permanent kit—one will suffice until you find a local supply.
13. Picture-hanging supplies—hooks, wire, and so on.
14. Your favourite mechanical kitchen gadgets, for example, garlic press, special biscuit cutters, and so on.

If you find an old list which says you should take things like stationery, holiday decorations and gift wrapping, disregard it. Times have changed and all these items are available. Do not, however, take religious decorations.

Things NOT to take
Do not bring anything that is irreplaceable or expensive (family heirlooms or antique furniture). Leave your TV set at home: it will not operate on Saudi current, and the cycles are different. Besides, there are thousands of high-quality TV sets available and they are cheap as well.

Contraband Items:
1. Alcoholic beverages—the consequences for smuggling or even drinking spirits, beer or wine can be jail, a very stiff fine, a flogging, or deportation. You will be thoroughly searched your first time through customs, although after a few years you will barely be questioned.
2. Narcotics.

3. Pornography—including nude works of art or pictures.
4. Non-Islamic religious articles and images.
5. Weapons (firearms, swords, bows and arrows), ammunition and fireworks. After living there for a while, you may be able to obtain a permit to bring a sporting firearm into the country, but do not take them in on the first trip. You will discover the gun souq, and if you are interested you can find some amazing antiques.
6. Arabic records—you can buy them there.
7. Playing cards—they can be bought in the country.
8. CB or other radio transmitters.
9. Recording devices which can be concealed on the person.
10. Anything made by firms on the boycott list (see pp. 63–64).

A final word
You should ship the maximum weight your company allows. While most items are available, they may not be to your taste and it takes a while to discover the best shopping areas. If you are going to a small town, selection will be minimal and excursions to a big city may be few and far between. Try to find out as much as you can about your living conditions and plan accordingly. Companies generally provide this information.

3
On Arrival

ARRIVAL INFORMATION

Airlines and airports

Saudi Arabian Airlines (Saudia) is the largest commercial carrier operating in the Middle East, with flights to Europe, North Africa, the Far East and North America. Saudia also serves twenty-three local airports. The airline is managed in conjunction with TWA, which has trained its pilots and personnel since it started operating in 1945. With a new, well-maintained fleet of aircraft, Saudia has an excellent safety record, is reliable, and is usually on schedule.

Many other major airlines have regular flights into the three international airports in the Kingdom (in Riyadh, Jiddah and Dhahran): TWA, Lufthansa, UTA (Air France), British Airways, Alitalia, KLM, Sabena, Swiss Air, Kenyan Airways, Egypt Air, Ethiopian Airways, Pan Am, Air Lanka, Air India, Singapore Air, Royal Jordanian Air and Gulf Air.

On your initial trip into the country it is essential that someone meet you: an expediter from your company, your sponsor, or a friend. Customs officials speak good English, immigration officials just barely enough, and porters none at all. Limousine drivers often speak English, taxi drivers almost never. Motorway signs into all three major cities are clearly marked in English and Arabic, but street signs, which are becoming more common, are only in Arabic. Unless you have taken some classes in Arabic, your pronunciation from your phrase book will most likely not be understood. In short, it can be a frightening experience arriving in the Kingdom without someone to guide you through the system and assist you with problems.

If you use the service of airport porters, be prepared to tip a minimum of SR 3 per bag: they will usually ask for more. Limousine service is the best choice for transportation into town as set rates are charged to specified zones. Numerous companies are available to choose from. Most ask for the fare in advance, and all will give receipts upon request. If you must use a taxi, agree on the fare with your driver before you leave the airport. Taxi fares can be quite expensive and meters are rare. Drivers may know only major buildings in the city but not street names. Here again, help from a Saudi is often valuable (more on taxis later in this chapter).

Hotels

There are now many hotel rooms available and competition for customers is strong, but it is still wise to reconfirm bookings. There are two ways to do this: have a local agent, colleague, or friend keep reconfirming your reservation at regular intervals right up to your arrival hour; and have him confirm your reservation with a substantial deposit for which he is given a receipt.

Registering with your embassy

It is important to register all members of your family with your embassy or consulate, and it should be done as soon as possible after arrival so that authorities have your full address if it is needed. While you are there, also register your passport number. If it were lost, that precaution would help considerably in having another reissued.

LIVING CONDITIONS

Foreigners are conspicuously isolated within compounds away from the community, and life can be difficult. Youssef M. Ibrahim described the life of foreigners in Saudi Arabia in the *New York Times* of 24th February 1980. Although written in 1980, Mr Ibrahim's description is still valid.

It is the unspoken law of Saudi Arabia that the people must be shielded from the hordes of aliens coming here to compensate for a shortage of Saudi labor. The practical answer to this view has been the foreigners' compounds. Saudi Arabia requires all companies that win contracts for projects here to build compounds for their foreign employees.

The segregated communities where foreigners are confined

stand out like modern-day ghettos. The more luxurious ones are behind walls. The modest ones are behind fences. Most are built of brick and concrete and have flower beds and swimming pools in the courtyards. Others (a few of the older ones) are depressing, prefabricated structures of cheap gray metal.

One compound dweller who has been here for three years talked of what she called the 'compound syndrome', a sort of numbing depression that slowly sets in. It affects housewives and bachelors the most, she said. The situation is worst for the wives. Unable to work unless they find employment within the compound, unable to drive a car anywhere because Saudi law forbids women to drive, unable to walk outside without being harrassed by young Saudis who think Western women are fair game, the women are prisoners of the compound. Their routine is reduced to visiting, playing bridge or tennis, gossiping, and waiting for their husbands to come home. They leave the compound a few times a week in organized trips by buses to the local bazaar or supermarket. Occasionally, there is an organized lunch in some hotel in town. But for the most part they stay in the compound.

While the picture painted here is harsh, foreign wives have a relatively wide variety of activities available to them if they will seek them out. The restrictions are difficult to adjust to and very confining, but those who are willing to make the effort to break out of the compound and explore the resources available in the society at large will have a much better chance of making a successful adjustment.

As mentioned before, women can go outside their compounds, but they must dress very modestly (preferably a long dress and a head scarf). If they ignore the whistles, the hecklers will soon go away.

IMPORTANT WARNINGS

Alcohol

Consumption of any alcoholic beverage is against Islamic law. *Sidiqi* is the name for homemade raw alcohol. This moonshine is dangerous to make or buy because it is impossible to tell if it is free of lethal impurities.

As the number of foreigners in Saudi Arabia grows, Saudis are

increasingly distressed at infractions of their laws and are growing
ever more strict and watchful, anxious to keep the country free of
what they consider to be degenerative influences. Formerly, foreigners were pretty much given free rein in their own compounds.
However, with the rise of traditionalism throughout the Middle
East, the system is undergoing change. Saudis will not tolerate a
breakdown of their values and therefore have been cracking down
harshly on the manufacture, sale or even possession of alcohol.
Police have the right to search private homes (without a warrant)
and have been known to do so in foreign (non-diplomatic) compounds. Penalties are severe—first, flogging (forty lashes, ad-
ministered in public), then jail, and finally deportation. The
incidence of public flogging is increasing, including some Americans, British and other foreigners. Ambassadors have all been
warned that they can no longer expect suspended sentences for
their citizens arrested on alcohol charges. Consular officials have
far less sympathy for citizens guilty of alcohol or drug possession
than for those inadvertently involved in a legal problem such as a
car accident.

Narcotics

Any foreigner who is caught with narcotics will be imprisoned, no
matter what age. No appeals for mercy have any impact, the outside
authorities have no power whatsoever in Saudi justice. If anyone
in your family has even an incipient problem with drugs, do not
take him or her to Saudi Arabia; the risks are simply too great.

Saudi justice

Penalties for all misdemeanours or crimes are extremely harsh,
with no leniency. Women can be stoned to death for adultery (this
punishment is very rare); repeated or large-scale theft may still be
punished with the loss of a hand after the third conviction (also a
very rare punishment). The result—rather understandably—is that
petty crime and street violence hardly exist in the Kingdom.

Crimes committed during the holy month of Ramadan are looked
upon much more seriously than at other times of the year. For
example, two men who robbed a bank during Ramadan were
executed for their crimes. It is extremely important for expatriates
to remember that legal judgments are made by Saudi and religious
law, not by foreign law. An embassy's officials can do no more
than guarantee that its citizens, if arrested, receive justice equal to

what Saudi nationals would receive under the same circumstances. They cannot intervene. It is absolutely imperative that all foreigners learn and follow Saudi laws; ignorance is never excusable. As noted in our discussion of the shari'a, Saudi laws are actually not so very different from ours: they are just enforced strictly and rapidly. Anyone who lives an orderly, conforming, law-abiding life has nothing to fear in Saudi Arabia. In fact, many people from crime-ridden Western cities find this security one of the great pleasures of living in Saudi Arabia.

Taking photographs
Foreigners are advised to be very cautious about taking pictures. If you want to take a picture of a Saudi, always ask permission first and be prepared for a refusal. The very scenes that we see as quaint, such as old or run-down houses or markets, are the ones that are certain to arouse resentment. Be particularly vigilant about religious pictures, for example, someone praying. Such pictures may actually constitute a religious misdemeanour.

Police are likely to put a possible offender in jail first and ask questions later. 'If you have to take photographs for the job,' one engineer said, 'my advice is: take a soldier with you; it is safer . . . and it saves a terrific amount of time if you can avoid hassles.'

Pictures that Westerners consider innocuous may be considered a security risk by the Saudi government, for example, pictures of airports or planes. All planes are owned by the government, and since the same airports serve both military and commercial purposes, they are carefully protected with tight security. Take no photographs anywhere near an airport, and take none of any planes.

HEALTH REQUIREMENTS

In the past, all visitors were required to have smallpox certificates: this is no longer a requirement. Cholera and yellow fever immunisations are necessary, however, for those arriving within five or six days from a country where there has been a recent outbreak of either disease. Those without necessary certificates will be vaccinated on arrival. Anyone coming directly from an infected area is subject to quarantine. All those applying to work in Saudi Arabia must fill out a complete health report.

TRANSPORTATION

Cars and driving

Cars are readily available—Japanese and European models at prices equivalent to those in the United States, and US models at slightly higher prices due to shipping costs. Secondhand cars are also available, but if you plan on buying one, be sure to have a mechanic check it over thoroughly first. Cars take a beating in Saudi Arabia. The air is heavy with salt in areas near the sea, the sun is relentless, and cars are scoured with sand in storms. Because of such an abusive environment, you should have your car well covered with a protective undercoating and lubricated frequently. Spare parts are available for the cars sold in Saudi Arabia; parts for other cars are often difficult to get.

There are enormous car souqs in all the major cities, and car buying can be quite an adventure. Take an experienced mechanic with you to the souq or be prepared to crawl under the cars yourself. You can take cars for a spin but not far away or for long. With the potential for severe punishment for theft, no one steals cars from the souq. All cars must have a safety inspection before they can be sold: this makes buying used cars less chancy than it once was.

One can import a car for personal use, subject to Saudi law, which at the moment states that such cars must be less than two years old. The freight costs of importing a car can be quite expensive. Enquire at the consulate for details. Because of the necessity for having cars and because of their high cost, some companies guarantee bank loans for their personnel and/or give them some other aid in securing a vehicle.

All cars must be registered, and you must have a letter of permission from your sponsor to be able to register a car in your name. If two people buy a car together, only one name may appear on the papers. The car registration paper, or 'blue book', must be in the car at all times. One interesting note is that in the Eastern Province, foreigners are not supposed to own four-wheel-drive vehicles. This can be circumvented, of course, with the help of a Saudi who can have the vehicle registered for you. (The reason for this rule is to prevent unlicensed drivers from taking carloads of pilgrims to the Hajj.)

Licence

The Saudi government does not recognise foreign or international driver's licences, but a foreigner needs a valid licence from home to apply for a Saudi one. Although women may own a car, they are not allowed to drive since the law states that anyone driving must have a Saudi licence, and licences are simply not issued to women. (Some women do drive within compounds.) Many people still use drivers even though Saudi roads are much improved and considerably less hazardous than before.

Insurance

Car insurance is not legally required, but good insurance is available at reasonable cost from several insurers, and it is foolish not to carry it. Since fines and compensation rates have fixed ceilings, there is no need to carry more than the maximum amount. Some companies provide their employees with less expensive group policies. Check with well-informed expatriates about the latest insurance information. You may also want to insure against fire and theft in a comprehensive policy.

Rules of the road

Driving is on the right, and speed limits are generally 30 km/hr in town (roughly 20 mph) and 100 to 120 km/hr on the motorways Saudis are like racing-car drivers behind the wheel. On twisting mountain roads, they make little compensation for the curves: they just change lanes and hope for the best. An intensive TV campaign about safe driving has had a considerable impact on driving habits and has brought down the highway death rate which, at one time, was so high that among the young men there was a negative population growth rate.

Intersections are an adventure. Traffic lights are placed far enough back from the intersection to allow opposing traffic through before the onslaught from the other direction arrives. Even though there are clearly marked lanes on the streets, cars squeeze in tightly next to each other at the light. When the light changes, it is like the start of a race, so be prepared. The wide streets marked for three lanes each way will usually have four lanes of traffic in each direction at the intersection—which then must squeeze back into three again.

Saudi drivers are aggressive and will watch to see if you are looking at them as you drive. Making eye contact usually means you are prepared to give way, and a Saudi will pull out in front of you. No matter how angry you become, never make obscene gestures to a Saudi. They understand every one of them and can become enraged and dangerous within seconds. Remember, you are a guest and have no right to be 'uppity'.

Traffic laws are enforced by a large and visible police force (many of them speak good English) and by periodic police checks at strategic points to catch and incarcerate offenders. Police also check registration and/or licences and—around the time of the Hajj—ID papers and/or passports. In fact, you should always carry your driver's licence, car registration and *igama*. You may be stopped and asked for these at any of the check-points.

Motorways are beautifully constructed, and highway design is, of course, supposed to prevent drivers going the wrong way on these high-speed thoroughfares. Unfortunately, illiterate drivers cannot always figure out the system and create terrible hazards.

Road construction and repair is a constant process. Motorways take a continual beating from overweight trucks. Secondary roads are being improved, and new roads are being cut through the desert to connect remote villages to the main roads. Construction projects in the cities are well marked and detours well planned, but they often take you far out of your way, which can be very annoying. Keep tabs on construction projects and drive a different route to avoid delays and problems.

Animals wandering the highway are the responsibility of the owner. Most people keep their animals at home at night, but occasionally there are still a few on the road. If you drive the open roads out of town at night, you will notice that Saudis drive with their lights on high beam all the time—even when they are right behind you—to be sure that they see stray animals in time to stop. Hitting a camel is a terrifying and sometimes fatal experience. You should also know that veiled women cannot judge speed very well and may walk out in front of you with their children in tow.

Accidents
Police investigation of accidents is much improved over earlier years, and judgments and penalties for accidents are usually quite fair. In the case of an accident, police generally take both drivers involved in an accident immediately to the police station for investigation (this includes passengers in a taxi). The vehicles are left just as they are, under guard, until responsibility has been

determined and compensation agreed upon. The process is time-consuming and often upsetting, given the unfamiliar language and surroundings, not to mention the normal jitters one feels following an accident. Call your consulate immediately if there has been any property damage or injury involved. One official offers this advice:

1. Try to settle at once with the other driver, especially if the accident is minor and/or the other driver is at fault. This will most likely save you both hours and trauma. If you cannot come to an agreement with the other driver, wait at the scene for the police. If the crowd (which always gathers) seems in a hostile mood, leave the scene but call the police immediately. Interestingly, the crowd will usually be divided 50/50 on who was in the wrong—regardless of the nationality of the drivers. When the police arrive, show them your Saudi ID card and ask permission to call the consulate (and/or your own office).
2. Obtain a police report before you take your car for any repair work, no matter how minor. Garages are checked regularly by the police to ensure that all vehicles being repaired have the necessary papers, so managers of the garages will not take on the work without the report. It is also important to know that only a licensed tow truck may tow a damaged vehicle.

Foreigners are urged not to involve themselves voluntarily in any accidents, even to give first aid or other help. There is now a 'good Samaritan' law but it is still better not to get involved.

Public transport

Taxis
Taxis are a popular means of transportation and can be found at hotels or contacted by phone. There are also shared taxis which follow set routes. Identifying marks include Arabic script on the wings or large red circles on the doors.

Negotiating fares with taxi drivers can either be an adventure or a nightmare, depending on your attitude and preparation. Taxis are not metered, so you will definitely want to settle the fare in advance. Ask around to determine the current rates beforehand and then stick to your price. Even after you have negotiated a price, the driver will undoubtedly insist on haggling for more at the end of the ride. Get out first and then pay, and if he grumbles too much, just put your money down on the seat and walk away. Of course, if you have a lot of baggage or have asked the driver to wait, you should pay more. Remember, though, that taxi drivers seldom speak English. Destination cards written in Arabic may not work either: the drivers are often dignified old men who cannot read and will be embarrassed at being shown cards they cannot decipher.

In Jiddah taxis officially have fixed rates, though drivers are likely to charge a good deal more, especially if they have been hailed at the airport or at a hotel. In the Dammam/Dhahran area the rates are fairly fixed; find out what they are for your destination before you get in the cab.

Limousines

Limousine companies are numerous and can be hired by the hour or by distance. You can find them at airports, at stands outside shopping centres, and in various places in town, or you can call them by phone. Limousines are usually kept cleaner and in better repair than taxis. They also charge set rates from zone to zone, simplifying things considerably for the expatriate. Most limousine drivers are Pakistanis and speak Urdu or English but rarely Arabic, so, again, there is no point in having destination cards.

It is probably not a wise idea for foreign women to ride unaccompanied in taxis, though limousines are usually safe. Saudi women are prohibited from riding alone in any public car.

Car rental

Rentals are available at airports and agencies in all cities at reasonable rates. Typical companies include Avis, Sahary, Budget, Hanco and many others. Visitors with a valid driver's licence in their own countries or an international driver's licence can rent cars for a limited time. Arrangements may be made from overseas or locally.

Buses

Buses offer an attractive alternative to taxis and limousines. SAPTCO (Saudi Arabian Public Transport Company) has developed an excellent urban and suburban bus system, which operates in all major cities. Both popular and successful, the bright red and blue chrome buses run often and on time, stopping every two hundred metres. Routes are well marked and fares cheap. (Taxis and limousines have now lowered their fares as a result of the bus service.)

Fares are paid on the honour system, with tickets or with cash. SAPTCO also operates between the major cities across the country, to Jordan, and on to Turkey.

A second bus line is owned and operated by a joint venture of Greyhound USA and two Saudi firms. Known as Greyhound–Taseco, these air-conditioned buses operate both within and between cities.

The rear sections of buses are reserved for women: they are separated from the men by a barrier and have their own entrances and exits. At dawn and mid-afternoon they are filled with school-girls; at dusk, with shoppers.

BANKING AND FINANCIAL MATTERS

There are numerous reliable banks in Saudi Arabia, many of them joint ventures with banks from other countries—for example, Saudi British Bank, Saudi Cairo Bank, or the Saudi American Bank. All banking in the Kingdom is conducted under Islamic laws, that is, no bank may accept or pay interest. As a result there is no such thing as a savings account.

Since Saudi Arabia is mainly a cash society, most expatriates do not bother with current accounts, preferring to send money home by bank draft (bought on payday) or direct deposit, keeping back only enough for monthly expenses. You can, of course, have a current account at the bank of your choice, and it is relatively easy to cash personal cheques when you are working in the Kingdom since the business establishment knows your firm will make good if you default.

Companies, of course, will need to keep bank accounts in the Kingdom. Employees are paid by cheque, and money must be quickly available for expenses, purchases, and so on. Some banks are open only in the mornings, but others are also open in the evenings, except for prayer times. Be sure to check with the bank about working hours.

It takes time to become accustomed to walking around with large wads of money, but you will be perfectly safe even in the most remote parts of the souq; no one will bother you or your cash. Money-changers are a legal banking alternative. They deal in foreign currencies and will issue, or cash, traveller's cheques and bank drafts in sterling or other currencies. The Al Rajhi Bank, one of the largest establishments in the Kingdom, is actually a money changer.

Major credit cards may be used at a few of the department stores and at hotels and large restaurants. The cards most often accepted are American Express, Diners Club and Visa. Over the past few years Carte Blanche, Eurocard and MasterCard have also been gaining acceptance.

There are no Saudi restrictions on taking money in or out of the country.

LANGUAGE

Arabs feel strongly about the superiority of Arabic because it is the language of the Qur'an. Since the Qur'an is believed to be the Word of God as revealed to Muhammad, Arabic is considered a divine language. The Qur'anic variety of the language is Classical Arabic; Modern Standard Arabic is nearly identical but with additional modern vocabulary.

Modern Standard Arabic is the accepted medium for all written material in the Arab world and is the language of the media and of oratory. Colloquial Arabic includes about fifteen dialects in the Arab world and is used for oral communication. The Saudi dialect is quite close to Classical Arabic because it has been exposed to few outside influences although the dialect on the west coast has been affected by Muslims visiting the holy cities over the centuries.

All Arabs love their language and are proud of the complexities of grammar and the flexibility of Arabic as a transmitter of thought. Poetry and eloquence are greatly honoured and respected. Although music is forbidden at any religious ceremony, poets are in great demand at weddings and celebrations, making up verses as they go to commemorate the occasion. Audiences, even illiterate, applaud and enjoy subtleties of rhyme and metre.

Although the Arabs consider their language one of their finest cultural achievements, most foreigners will unfortunately never know it well enough to appreciate its finer points. It is a difficult language for Westerners to master, partly because of its complexity and partly because of the pronunciation of several sounds made far back in the mouth and throat.

Learning at least a few courtesy phrases is an excellent way to extend friendship and make a good impression. When you speak of the future, add *inshallah* (if God wills), and when you meet someone's small child, say *bismillah* (in the name of God).

Other useful phrases include

Hello	*Marhaba*
Good morning	*Sabaah al-khayr*
Good evening	*Masa' al-khayr*
Goodbye	*Ma'a salaama*
Welcome	*Ahlan wa sahlan*
Thanks	*Shukran*
You're welcome/ not at all	*'Afwan*

See also the glossary for the Arabic words and phrases used in this book.

4
Doing Business

FOREIGN BUSINESS VENTURES—Success or failure?

His Excellency Yousif Al-Hamdan, Deputy Minister of Commerce
for Saudi Arabia, summarised what made for success—or the lack
of it—among foreigners in his country during a speech in the
United States (US—Arab Trade Seminar, Los Angeles, spring
1980). Although written some time ago, his analysis is still
applicable.

Foreign businessmen experience difficulty and failure when they
assume that:

1. the Saudi Arabian market is just like any other market;
2. they do not have to compete if their product is good; and
3. the potential buyers are too unsophisticated to know differences
   in quality and price.

In sum, failure is the result of neglecting to take the Saudi market
seriously enough to do the kind of thorough investigation that
success in the market demands.

Al-Hamdan then proceeded to outline steps to successful foreign
business ventures:

1. A careful study of the market.
2. The formation of a partnership, based on trust on both sides,
   with a competent and congenial Saudi Arabian colleague or
   firm.
3. The awareness by both partners of the problems the other must
   deal with and of the inevitable hurdles that both sides will have
   to overcome on the way to consummation of any sales or
   agreements.

4. The willingness to make a *long-term commitment* and engage in careful, steady follow-up. Reputations, on which business success depends, fly across the desert with lightning speed. Arabs have been harmed by short-term, casual, and unfulfilled commitments and avoid them assiduously.

5. An understanding of Saudi Arabia's seriousness about moving ahead without gambling away the nation's future. Oil is a precious but expendable resource. The country is serious about spending its revenues wisely for the future.

6. Recognition of the fact that for Saudis, business is a very personal matter. Directness and willingness to make a commitment mean far more to a Saudi than advanced degrees or fancy corporate titles.

The competition for Saudi contracts is keen. In the past the United States has taken a large share of the business, but now France, Britain, Germany, Japan, Sweden, Canada and South Korea, among other countries, are making significant inroads into the Saudi market. However, for anyone doing business in Saudi Arabia, an important factor to bear in mind is the Arab boycott (blacklist) which is a part of the Arab–Israeli dispute. As long as the conflict continues, so will the boycott, whatever outsiders think of it. Arabs consider the boycott a 'function of the absence of peace'. Theoretically, at least, companies are not boycotted because they do business with Israel but rather if they

1. make direct investments in Israel;
2. licence a product there; or
3. manufacture directly in Israel.

Firms avoiding these restrictions can do business simultaneously in Israel and the Arab world, and some do. Arabs often bend their own rules, depending on circumstances. For example, the Ford Motor Company was excluded from Saudi Arabia because of the boycott, but in 1988 Ford cars were once again on the Saudi market. The reason for this change is anyone's guess: perhaps there was a softening of heart.

Companies on the list include Coca-Cola, Bulova, Helena Rubenstein, Helene Curtis, Sears and Zenith. Some UK firms include Austin and Philco. Other companies have been on the list but are once again doing business, such as Leyland, Ford, Sony,

Xerox, Hitachi, Sharp, Land Rover and Jaguar. A few companies have always operated in both the Arab countries and Israel, such as American Express, Hilton and TWA.

You should avoid trying to import items made by boycotted companies. Although detailed information about companies on the list is not public, enquiries regarding the status of specific companies are accepted by the Commercial Office of the Saudi Embassy in London (tel: (071) 589 7246).

Still another problem the Saudis have—and which any of the oil-producing countries has with industrial nations—is that they are on the horns of a dilemma. As Abdallah R. Dabbaugh, a former Saudi Commercial Counsellor, put it:

> If we invest in the U.S., we are trying to buy it; if we do not, we are not recycling our surplus dollars and so are hurting the U.S. economy. If we increase our production of oil, we are trying to ride higher prices; if we do not, we are blackmailing!

KEY BUSINESS ORGANISATIONS

Central Planning Board
The Central Planning Board, established in 1964, has a staff of about two hundred and is answerable to the king. Its functions include undertaking economic analyses and issuing reports, preparing development plans and estimating the funds that will be required, assisting agencies with planning projects, and providing technical advice to the king.

Petromin (General Petroleum and Minerals Organisation)
Petromin, a national petroleum company, was created in 1962 to formulate and execute projects for the development of petroleum, gas, petrochemicals and minerals, and to manage Saudi Arabia's increasing participation in and control over ARAMCO. It handles refining, pipelines, storage, power generation and domestic and international marketing. Petromin's annual output rose by approximately 500 per cent in the Third Five-Year Plan alone.

Sabic (Saudi Arabian Basic Industrial Corporation)
SABIC is an example of how the Saudi government has blended long-range planning and investment with the use of public and

private sources of finance. It was established in 1976 to provide capital for heavy-industry projects and to serve as the co-ordinating organisation for these projects. SABIC itself is funded through joint-venture partners, the government and commercial loans. It administers the new industrial complexes at Jubail and Yanbu, including steel, fertiliser and petrochemical plants, and has plans for other industries such as glass, cement, car parts and metallurgy.

Sama (Saudi Arabian Monetary Agency)
SAMA is, in effect, Saudi Arabia's central bank, regulating the money supply and the value of the riyal, supervising all of the country's banking, promoting economic development, and reviewing proposals for funds. SAMA is reluctant to add more banks to the system, which in 1983 already included eleven commercial banks, most of which are affiliated with banks in Europe, the United States, and the United Kingdom.

JOINT VENTURES

The Saudi government offers significant incentives to joint ventures such as low-cost land, electricity, loans, tax holidays, exemptions, and protective 'buy Saudi' procurement regulations. Some of the most promising opportunities for foreign investors are in health, telecommunications, computers and data processing, agriculture, maintenance, and personnel support services.

Making arrangements with local agents or partners has long been the customary way for foreigners to do business in the Middle East. Now, however, Saudis—and other oil exporters—are determined to curb the influence of local agents, preferring joint ventures instead. Joint ventures require a fixed minimum per cent of Saudi participation and various bid and performance guarantees.

A good joint venture is an excellent arrangement and in any case, a foreign contractor must have a Saudi partner or sponsor if he wishes to succeed. Saudi officials vastly prefer working directly with company officials to dealing through middlemen, and they like face-to-face arrangements with the principals involved. Your Saudi partner or the company's expediter can often move the slow wheels of government as no foreigner can, most likely because many government officials moonlight as businessmen, a practice that is quite legal.

Prices, however, must be kept competitive—the days of

astronomical bids are long past. As part of a current anti-inflation drive, Saudis are curbing the scale and size of their projects, postponing some, trimming others, and cancelling some altogether.

GOVERNMENT FINANCING

Wealthy Saudis are making fortunes in real estate. Anyone who owns a plot of land can take advantage of the government housing programme whereby the state finances 70 per cent of the building cost with no interest, and payment is spread over twenty years— the down payment to the builder is an outright gift. As a result of the government's generosity, the major cities are quite overbuilt. Compounds of homes built for foreigners are standing empty and rents have plummeted (a real boon to outsiders).

Incentives of the same kind are set up for the purchase of agricultural machinery, fertiliser and livestock: the government absorbs half the price and finances the rest, without interest. Many farms have flourished, but others have been started only to be abandoned, the expensive pivot sprinkler systems left to corrode in the harsh desert air.

Industrial ventures are also promoted with extensive government aid. Saudi businessmen can apply to a special fund that lends half the necessary capital for twenty-five years without interest and grants exemption from taxes for five years. A new generation of Saudis, mainly educated abroad, is going into industrial investment, often with foreign partners. (Some 7,000 Saudi students are in the United States at this time. The number in both the United States and the United Kingdom has declined since the early 1980s. Altogether, about 10,000 male students are studying abroad, many of whom are in Egypt as well as in Europe.)

Foreign contractors should be aware that the Saudi government is much less generous with money and much more exacting about contracts than it was when oil income seemed unlimited. Oil revenues declined (from $109 billion in 1981 to $50 billion in 1986) and will probably never again reach the previous heady levels. You can expect a careful and detailed scrutiny of all proposals.

Saudi Arabia is also sending vast amounts of money to other countries. Arab League funds are helping both Arab and African countries to buy petroleum and other needed products and to secure development funds. The Saudi Fund for Economic Development sends billions of riyals to developing countries, including substantial emergency contributions to famine areas in Somalia, Ethiopia and Sudan. The Islamic Development Bank gives interest-free loans since Islam prohibits the charging of interest on loans, as stated before.

TIME

The matter of pace is for many Westerners the most difficult adjustment to the Middle East. If you are in a hurry in the Middle East, do not bother. The same sentiment is expressed in the well-known Arabic proverb: 'Haste comes from the Devil.' Arabs in general dislike a sense of time pressure or urgency. Patience is the key to successful adaptation in Saudi Arabia. If you can wait patiently for an appointment, you will be off to a positive start. When it is your turn, your Saudi host will be extremely courteous— and will expect the same from you no matter how tried your patience. Visible annoyance will only be counterproductive, perhaps permanently so.

Calendar

Saudi Arabia uses both the Islamic and the Western calendar. The Islamic calendar began with the Prophet's **Hegira** (emigration) from Mecca to Medina in AD 622. Hegira dates are marked AH (Anno Hegirae—after the Hegira). The year 1989, for example, is the latter part of the year 1409 AH and the beginning of 1410. The Islamic year is divided into twelve lunar months which average 29½ days, making the Islamic year eleven days shorter than the Western year. Therefore, Muslim holidays fall on earlier dates every year. For example, Ramadan was on April 7 in 1989, on March 27 in 1990 and on March 16 in 1991. Similarly, the Hajj also comes earlier every year.

All offices have double calendars so you can easily find the equivalent date. You may see the abbreviations ce or bce in newspapers or books—this is the equivalent of AD and BC and means 'common era', not 'Christian Era'.

Telling time

As is the case in much of the world, Saudi Arabia uses the twenty-four hour clock rather than twelve. Thus, 8:00 pm is written as 2000 and 1:00 pm as 1300. Although Greenwich mean time has been officially adopted, there is one aspect of Arab time that is confusing for foreigners. The Arab day begins at sunset. This means that the night of Monday precedes Monday rather than follows it. It may help to think of it as the eve of Monday, much as we speak of New Year's Eve.

All of Saudi Arabia is in the same time zone (GMT plus three hours). However, companies in the Eastern Province add an extra hour—GMT plus four hours in the winter and GMT plus five hours in the summer (April to September)—since that area of the country is at the eastern boundary of the time zone. Clarify this after your arrival.

Holidays and weekends
Government and business recognise only two official holidays:

1. Eid al Fitr celebrates the end of Ramadan and lasts three to five days, sometimes longer; plus, most offices close two days before Ramadan.
2. Eid al Adha, the Feast of the Sacrifice, is the highlight of the pilgrimage to Mecca and Medina and often lasts about four days.

Foreigners are advised to avoid making business appointments and business trips from a few days before to a few days after both the above holidays and during the time of the Hajj. It is also wise, as mentioned earlier, to cut back, where possible, on activities during the entire month of Ramadan. Business slows as the month progresses, eapecially when Ramadan falls in the summer.

In addition to these two national holidays, there are a multitude of other widely observed local and religious holidays throughout the year. The importance of obtaining and following a current Islamic calendar should be obvious.

Holidays are not, however, the only poor times for doing business; summer qualifies as well. Many Saudi businessmen and senior government officials flee to cool resorts in the mountains or to Europe. In addition, Jumada I and II, the fifth and sixth Islamic months, are budget months for government offices. Gaining access to top planners and executives may be difficult during that period. On a daily basis prayer times may impede business, and for those who go to a nearby mosque rather than praying in their offices, each prayer session may be half an hour longer.

Throughout the Muslim world weekends are Thursday and

Friday, not Saturday and Sunday. Most foreign businesses close Friday instead of Sunday, partly out of courtesy, partly for efficiency. Try to avoid arriving in Saudi Arabia on Thursdays or Fridays if possible—you may find no one to meet you or transport you home. Also be prepared to be generally self-sufficient for those two days—very little happens.

Business and working hours

Business and working hours are somewhat flexible and vary from place to place according to the time of year. In general, however, the best time to make appointments is late morning, after the day has begun but before it gets hot. Most offices are open five days a week (closing on Thursdays and Fridays—some organisations still open for a half-day on Thursdays). Generally, offices are open from 0830 to 1300 or 1400 (8:30 am to 1:00 or 2:00 pm), then again from 1630 to 2000 (4:30 pm to 8:00 pm). Actually, a great deal of work is done between 2000 and midnight, when it is cooler. Shop hours are approximately the same, with lunch between noon and 1600. Banks, however, tend to close for the day at noon, and many government offices close for the day at 1400.

Total working hours are officially set at no more than eight hours a day or forty-eight hours a week. During Ramadan six working hours a day is maximum (thirty-six per week), excluding times of rest, prayer, and meals on certain shifts. These rules can be bent or stretched in some circumstances: for example, a ministry may increase the total daily working hours to nine, though never with more than five at a stretch. For some kinds of work (watchmen, janitors, and so on) and at certain peak times (inventory time or high-pressure periods of various sorts), workers may put in overtime, which must be paid at one to one- and-a half times the normal rate. Overtime pay is also required for work on holidays and rest days.

COMMUNICATIONS

The telephone system

Saudi Arabia now has one of the most sophisticated telephone systems in the world. Not long ago, phone calls to cities outside the country could easily take three or four days if they went through at all, but that has changed drastically. In December 1977 the

Saudis signed with Bell of Canada the biggest telecommunications contract in history, involving a gigantic network of microwave towers, coaxial cables, earth satellite stations and, initially, two million telephones.

When the programme started, only seven Saudi cities were connected by phone. Within a scant twenty-seven months that number had skyrocketed to eighty-four cities and villages. The original goal of two million phones was upgraded to four or five million. The engineering problems have been prodigious, but the job is progressing with incredible speed.

The same service and emergency numbers apply throughout the country:

Long distance calls	900 (for operator assistance only)
International	901
Traffic accidents	993
Directory enquiries	905
Telephone repairs	904
Ambulance	997
Fire	998
Police	999
Time	963

Other dialling codes
Saudi Arabia	010 966
followed by	
Abha	7
Abqaiq	3
Bukayriyah	6
Dammam	3
Dhahran	3
Hail	6
Hawiyah	2
Hofuf	3
Jiddah	2
Jubail	3
Layla	1
Mecca	2
Medina	4
Qatif	3
Rabigh	2

Ras Tanurah	3
Riyadh	1
Shaqra	1
Tabuk	4
Taif	2
Yanbu	4

followed by customer's number.

Please take acount of business and prayer times when you make your call. Saturday to Thursday morning is the working week in Saudi Arabia. Time difference is three hours later than Greenwich Mean Time.

Telex, telegrams and mail

Foreign organisations operating in Saudi Arabia have access to the Mark-3 telex service, based in two computer centres in the United States and one in The Netherlands. Pending approval by the Saudi Ministry of Posts, Telegraphs and Telecommunications, users can connect a computer terminal with the network by dialling the local telephone number and operating the computer by keyboard. Telex and fax machines are used by most companies and are available in the major hotels.

Messages may be sent by telegram, but mail is usually quicker. Air mail between Saudi Arabia and Europe takes four to five days and between Saudi Arabia and the United States, eight to ten days. For mailing purposes use your post office address, not your street address. Stamps are not always available, but letters are franked at the post office. Because the mail service is relatively slow, many companies use courier services, such as SNAS—DHL or Skypak.

Sending and receiving parcels is risky business. The best advice is to avoid doing so altogether: high duties on packages are common, for those that arrive at all. Although there is no duty on used goods, there may be high 'clearing costs'. Retrieving parcels at the post office is also extremely tedious.

Whether entering or leaving Saudi Arabia, mail is subject to censorship. You are a guest, and it is not a good idea to write anything derogatory about the country, the people, your work, or (most of all) the Islamic religion. Matters involving security or adverse conditions of life or work should not be mentioned either in letters or on the phone.

English-language newspapers and periodicals

The best-known English-language daily newspapers are *Arab News*, *Saudi Gazette* and *Riyadh Daily*. *The Saudi Review* is a translation of Arabic newspapers in periodical format. In addition, the *Saudi Economic Review*, a weekly review in English of Saudi Arabian economic and business activity, publishes various government tenders, new regulations and other useful economic information.

Although somewhat expensive, international editions of *Time*, *Newsweek*, the *International Herald Tribune* (from Paris), the *London Times*, the *Beirut Daily Star* and some other publications are regularly available. Information and pictures in these publications are sometimes blacked out or reworded by censors. Many editions of magazines from various countries are readily available (also often censored).

Paperbacks in English are much sought after: the supply is limited and the prices are high. Books in French and German are also available in bookstores.

BUSINESS MECHANICS

Currency

The unit of currency, as mentioned earlier, is the Saudi riyal, (SR). Riyals are subdivided into one hundred **halalah**, but due to inflation, the halalah has so little value that it is often omitted in pricing or giving change. Denominations of notes and coins are as follows:

Paper notes: 1, 5, 10, 50, 100 SR
Coins: 5, 10, 25, 50 halalahs

The current (September 1991) exchange rate is: SR 6.32 = £UK1.00.

For many years paper money was forbidden by law; all transactions were done with silver, gold or foreign currency. In 1953, out of consideration for the Mecca pilgrims (who had a hard time carrying so much gold and silver with them), paper 'pilgrims' receipts were issued. The receipts were a great success and were gradually adopted for use in all transactions. In 1961 the government officially issued paper currency and took the receipts out of circulation. Since 1982, paper money has been imprinted with likenesses of the king, a break with Islamic tradition which forbids the making of 'graven images'.

Accounting and taxes

Foreign companies usually keep books in both Arabic and their own language because financial statements in foreign languages are not acceptable to the tax department. Books must be presented at the end of each tax year to the Department of Zakat and Income Tax, which is headquartered in Jiddah but which has six branch offices elsewhere in the country.

There is no set tax year. Businesses are taxed every twelve months from the time the company is established, as based on the company's own records. Tax regulations change periodically, and you should consult a local accountant for current guidelines.

Insurance and interest

When a Muslim says inshallah, which is in almost every conversation, it is not an empty phrase, despite its frequency. Since they believe that nothing happens without God's willing it, many devout Muslims feel that insurance is impious and defies Allah. Nevertheless, there are now insurance companies in Saudi Arabia. Despite this, you will find that business inventories are often uninsured.

In 1960 a number of regulations were passed to govern a fund (known as GOSI) to cover compensation for injury, disability, old age and death. Foreign managers should read these regulations carefully because they differ in some ways from those in their own countries. Only Saudi citizens now pay into this fund, and any company with Saudi employees must be sure to follow the regulations on collections.

Labour laws

Labour laws are clearly and extensively spelled out in a manual available from the Ministry of Labour. Anyone going to Saudi Arabia in a managerial position should study the Saudi labour laws, which are periodically updated. A work permit is required for all foreign nationals, and all workers must have a contract that states conditions of employment, end-of-service payments and severance pay, medical insurance, leave and holidays. Any worker has the right to read the labour law manual and to go to the labour board to complain about mistreatment, lack of payment of salary, and so on.

Baksheesh

The word **baksheesh** refers to a tip or gratuity given for a service. Foreigners often misunderstand this Middle Eastern custom. Most firms—and individuals too—have what is sometimes called a 'petty cash payroll', which refers to the 5 or 10 per cent expected baksheesh one pays to have things installed, moved, approved, certified, released, repaired, and so on, in the course of daily life. It is necessary to pay baksheesh to get most things done, just as it is in many other parts of the world.

Naturally, if you keep servants up late for a big party, you pay them extra, but that is not baksheesh. If someone guards your car, carries your parcels, opens a gate, or otherwise serves you, you should give a coin or two: that is not baksheesh either. Baksheesh is usually given after the business dealing is over, to say thank you and to create good relationships for future dealings. It may be alluded to or hinted at but is never openly and explicitly offered or asked for. Baksheesh is not necessarily money: it can be a gift or a favour. Business is conducted on a personal basis, and baksheesh helps develop the personal relationship. This personal nature of business is a difficult concept for Westerners to grasp; they often confuse the Western concept of bribe and the Arabic concept of baksheesh. Although the two may seem the same on the surface, they are not. A bribe is a sum of money offered before negotiations ever get started. Bribery can be dangerous and can, in some cases, even lead to jail. *Baksheesh* enhances your business reputation; bribery damages it, and in Saudi Arabia, business is everybody's business; in other words, everyone will know what you have done.

Gifts are still different. A modest gift is often given after a second or third business meeting. It should not be of great value and should never be an advertising item. Some small novelty or product from the visitor's home country or hometown is acceptable and appreciated—perhaps a little tool or an electronic gadget or item for the recipient's desk.

Bureaucracy

Red tape is always frustrating, but the wise Western businessman will roll with the punches and relax. Firms should bear in mind the need for flexibility and patience when they select personnel for assignments in the Arab world. Those who fight the system will only lose—and it will not do their reputation any good either. The

Saudi bureaucracy is bigger and older than any of us and is not going to be pushed about by some foreigner.

Business cards

Business cards are essential in Saudi Arabia because they provide data that may not be available anywhere else—Arabs often have unlisted telephone numbers and private addresses. Your file of cards becomes your private business directory. Cards are printed in two languages, your own on one side and Arabic on the other.

You should present your own card immediately on meeting an Arab, making sure the Arabic side is presented face upwards. He will return your courtesy by presenting his card with your language facing upwards. If your company name is well known, you do not need to have it translated. If not, the addition of a phonetic transliteration of the company name is a helpful and courteous gesture.

Finding personnel

Finding personnel is, of course, a major problem. Saudis look for real competence and are disgusted with bumbling or incompetent representatives. Foreign firms are expected to send only good men, not people of questionable ability. They will be in a competitive world, and Saudis can tell at fifty paces if they are being patronised. The demand for Saudi personnel, particularly at the executive level, is enormous, and even new university graduates command top salaries. There is no formal system for finding personnel: it has to be done through contacts, such as current employees, clients, marketing officers or others. Thus, a new firm entering Saudi Arabia should send its personnel man out to the country as early as possible to start making contacts, to talk and drink coffee with people, to develop ties. The process can be discouraging: one or two good leads may take weeks. Once again, patience will be called for.

BUSINESS ETIQUETTE

Personal but not private

We have mentioned the personal nature of doing business with Saudis; its importance cannot be overemphasised. A Saudi will not care how good your proposal is if he does not know and trust you. This means many cups of coffee or tea and a number of meetings with no mention of business at all. But this is not just idle chatting. All the while your Saudi host is assessing your trustworthiness, getting to know you as a person and evaluating your competence. The establishment of a relationship takes a lot of time, but without it, you may as well pack your bags and go home.

Do not be surprised, however, if your personal appointments are not private. There will most likely be a number of other people in the room, two telephones ringing and constant interruptions. Arabs are enormously private in their homes and about their personal lives; their souls are inviolate. Once they are in the public arena, however, privacy means nothing. You may think your business is confidential; your Saudi host probably will not. Impatience or demands for privacy will only hurt your case. Instead, relax, have tea with everybody, join the conversation. When your host signals that it is time to talk business, do so openly and freely. If you cannot stand the confusion, try to work your way closer to your host and whisper a word into his ear now and then, between interruptions.

Confidentiality will likely increase when the time comes to actually sign a contract, and you will probably work one-to-one. Mid-level administrators are often called in at that point—often Palestinians, Pakistanis, Egyptians or Yemenis. Paperwork is considered routine and is therefore left to imported workers. Saudis are the élite: their job is to mastermind, to make contacts and decisions, but then to bow out when it comes to details. Sometimes these foreign workers engage in 'power games', which can be not only annoying but make the paperwork even more tedious. It is a different way of doing business from what Westerners are accustomed to, but it works. In any case, you have no choice.

Rank and protocol
Both class and rank are quite important to Arabs despite the Muslim concept of equality before God. This becomes rather clear at doorways as business colleagues sort themselves out by status: the senior-ranking men go through first, followed by the next in the hierarchy, and so on. However, as a guest, you will probably be ushered through first.

In a list of Arab loyalties, the extended family ranks first, followed by friends, then the Arab/Muslim community, the country, and finally non-Arab Muslims. Outsiders, no matter what their rank, importance or financial status, fall well behind these five, especially those who are non-Muslim. However, a guest is a guest at all times and will be accorded full courtesies whether Muslim or not—so long as that guest is behaving within the Arab code of etiquette.

Invitations

If you invite a colleague to a restaurant or for coffee, be prepared to be refused at least once. The general rule is to refuse first, then accept a cup of coffee, an invitation to lunch, precedence through the door, and so on. Generally, whoever issues the invitation also picks up the bill. Everyone else will offer, even if you invited them, so you must persist. As with any generality, there are exceptions to custom, especially among younger Saudis, but follow this rule of thumb until you become accustomed to Saudi culture.

Body language

Because of their desert heritage, Saudis have a noticeably different sense of space than those who come from non-Arab countries. Standing in line is unheard of; whoever reaches a watering hole first—or a taxi—wins. The same is true of conversations. Interrupting is not offensive if the person doing it has an urgent reason for doing so or has higher status. Arabs need very little personal space around them. Their conversational distance (about ten inches) is about half of what is normally comfortable for most Northern Europeans and Americans and perhaps a third of what is comfortable for Asians. (Southern Europeans and Latin Americans are comfortable with a conversation distance similar to that of Arabs.) It is important not to draw back, however; Saudis will interpret your withdrawal as a rebuff. In addition, Arabs engage in a lot of body contact. They like to tap a person's shoulder or rest a hand on a hand or an arm on an arm (though Saudis do this less than other Arabs). Such physical contact is taken as an assurance of attention or a means of emphasis, a way to make a point or express a feeling. But it is never done obviously, as slapping the back or prodding the ribs to emphasise a point or a joke. Men frequently hold hands, embrace warmly in public, or kiss one another on the cheek. An American reports having seen a burly soldier move his gun to the other hand so he could walk hand in hand down the street with a fellow soldier. This is the way of life there and does not have the overtones that it does in some cultures. When talking, Saudis stand not only with their faces close together but with their bodies close as well, though not touching. Again, try not to draw back.

A sense of space can also be observed in the large size of Saudi offices and even more so in their philosophy of 'out of sight, out of mind'. Once you had disappeared into the shifting sands of the desert, no one thought of you again until you reappeared. The tradition is essentially intact today. To do business with an Arab, you, or your representative, need to maintain a constant physical presence. If you do not, little is likely to be done, and someone else may take your place.

Hands and eyes are used deliberately and carefully in conversation. Talking with one's hands, gesticulating wildly, is considered impolite. Foreigners should train themselves to keep both hands quiet as they talk lest their gestures be misunderstood or, unwittingly, be in bad taste.

Muslims keep the left hand for private functions and use the right for everything public, which includes eating, shaking hands, or passing a document (or money or a gift) across a table. Non-Muslims should be extremely careful to do the same, whether or not they are right-handed.

Suggestions for the foreign business executive

1. Appearance is important. Dress neatly and conservatively. A messy, slovenly appearance is taken as a sign of disrespect.
2. Your approach should be calm, low-key, and unhurried. A flashy, noisy, boisterous visitor will seldom win trust—or a contract.
3. Let the Saudis take the lead in public announcements of contracts, agreements, changes of personnel, or whatever. They do not like boasting and are turned off by premature publicity about business transactions which they may not consider completed or ready to be announced. Their attitude is that anything important will be known in good time.
4. Try to be comfortable with silences in conversations; they are frequent and normal. The Arabs have a saying: 'God gave man two ears and one tongue so he could listen twice as much as he could talk.' You must be able, however, to discern between a long and thoughtful silence and the end of the interview. Usually this is easy because most meetings end with yet another cup of coffee.
5. Be judicious about discussion of the future. Saudis think it is

bad luck to talk too much about the future, which will unfold according to God's will, not man's. How can mortals say what lies ahead? Openly expressed plans, hopes and intentions for the future make them uncomfortable. Obviously, they make future plans, but they feel it is unwise to announce the future far in advance.

6. Your business behaviour should be formal. Sometimes foreigners offend by smoking, crossing their legs, or other subtle actions that express relaxation and are inappropriate in certain circumstances. The best policy, as in all cross-cultural situations, is to watch others and not be the first to do anything.

7. Never underestimate an Arab. Assume that all of them are every bit as bright as you: many of them will be more so. Remember that Saudis have been traders since before the seventh century, when Mecca was the centre of a far-flung trading world. Even without formal education, they have always been shrewd at business. When you add excellent educations to that inherent shrewdness, they present formidable business competition. They do it with grace, however. Furthermore, they are far more accustomed to Western businessmen than most of us are to them. After all, Arabs have been working with the West for many decades, and many have a superior command of your language. To underestimate them is simply not wise.

8. Arabs are an emotional people. Their dignity is important to them, as is their personal honour, and they guard both jealously. This can make them appear touchy sometimes; they often feel slighted when no offence is intended. Nearly always their hurt feelings relate to their sense of personal honour which, in turn, reflects on their family honour.

9. Westerners are sometimes more free and informal in their use of language than is appropriate when dealing with Saudis. The use of swear words (even as tame as 'damn') or coarse language downgrades the speaker to a degree that few outsiders realise. Throughout the Muslim world, no man of culture uses such words. Using that kind of language, even though it is quite common in Western offices, will undercut your status. Even more serious are the mildly disparaging remarks, often intended to be humorous or jocular, that Westerners often exchange with their work colleagues and friends, such as, 'Don't be an idiot.' These may be interpreted by an Arab as

a personal insult, perhaps dishonouring his whole family. Insults to a man's honour are virtually unforgivable among Arabs. Anyone going to the Arab world should guard against giving inadvertent offence.

10. Be very careful not to contradict, scold, or criticise people in public, including colleagues from your own country, but especially don't criticise Arabs. Not only are such actions an insult to a Saudi's honour and dignity, but they will cause you to lose face as well.

11. Be respectful and courteous in all your dealings with Saudis. For example, don't terminate a meeting or conversation too rapidly. When a man leaves your office (or your home), walk with him at least to the door of the building or, better yet, to the car, with smiles, bows, and polite comments spoken with warm feeling. Shaking hands at the door to your own office and turning back to your desk without seeing your guest out, at least part way, will be interpreted as brusque and rude. Time spent on good manners and hospitality is time gained.

12. Spend whatever time is necessary to learn your material backwards and forwards—in other words, do your homework. Since Saudis are accustomed to learning by memorising, they tend to have excellent memories and use them well. The Western executive shuffling through his papers to find a date, a number or a fact is something of a figure of fun to Saudis.

Recommended resources for business executives

Readers should seek advice from their foreign offices, international banks, the Saudi embassies in their countries or whatever sources they find available, including Saudi students.

For British businessmen the following resources are recommended:

1. **Department of Trade and Industry**
   British business: DTI weekly export and industrial news magazine.
   Committee for Middle East Trade: area advisory group to the DTI.
   Export Credits Guarantee Department: insurance and access to cheap export finance.
   Export Intelligence Service: rapid circulation of specific and general market and economic information.

Product Data Store: product and industry-based information on overseas markets.

Saudi Arabia desk: wide range of market information.

Simplification of International Trade Procedures (SITPRO): information to help reduce exporting costs and improve customer service.

Statistics and Market Intelligence Library: wide collection of trade information.

2. **Foreign and Commonwealth Office**, Middle East Department, can give an update on the political situation.

3. **The British Embassy in Riyadh.** Business enquiries will be referred to offices in Jiddah or Al Khobar where appropriate. General background briefings may be sought from the main Commercial Department.

4. **The Saudi Embassy.** The Commercial Office in London can provide the Charter for the Development Fund and the Investment Code for Saudi Arabia, as well as other essential documents.

5. **Arab–British Chamber of Commerce:** range of information and other services for all concerned with Arab— British trade.

6. **ARAMCO's Industrial Development Department.** Its local office in the Eastern Province is willing to help people from other companies with such general information as basic data about water availability, names of representatives, and so on.

7. **BBC External Services** broadcast throughout the world in English and thirty-six other languages. New developments in British industry, science and technology are featured prominently in the programmes.

8. **Central Office of Information** can provide overseas publicity for British exporters via government information services.

9. **The Middle East Association** aims to promote two-way trade with Arab countries and with Afghanistan, Ethiopia, Iran and Turkey by means of information and advice.

10. **Banks.** The International Divisions of major banks prepare economic reports which are generally available free of charge.

11. **Chambers of Commerce** (London, Birmingham and Manchester). These organisations usually hold market information which is available to members.

12. **Other sources.** Many public libraries in the United Kingdom hold commercial information useful to the exporter.

The following antonomous Saudi government agencies may also be of help:

1. **Contractors Classification Committee,** Riyadh; **General Electricity Organisation,** Riyadh. These are responsible for funnelling government finance to private electricity companies and co-ordinating them into regional organisations.
2. **Islamic Development Bank,** Jiddah, finances development projects in other Muslim countries.
3. **Petromin,** Riyadh, has responsibility for the refining and commercialisation of oil. Subsidiaries:
   Petrolube
   Petroserve (project services)
   Petroship (tanker fleet)
   Petrojet (bulk storage of refined product)
   Petronal, London and Houston (international marketing of oil and gas)
   Petromark (marketing)
4. **Public Investment Fund,** Riyadh, finances Saudi Basic Industries Corporation joint ventures and key private industrial companies.
5. **Real Estate Development Fund,** Riyadh, provides cheap finance to Saudi nationals towards the cost of building accommodation.
6. **Royal Commission for Jubail and Yanbu,** Riyadh, is responsible for the development of new industrial complexes at Jubail and Yanbu.
7. **Saudi Arabian Red Crescent Society,** Riyadh, is the Islamic equivalent of the Western Red Cross Society.
8. **Saline Water Conversion Corporation,** Riyadh. The Minister of Agriculture is the Chairman ex officio.
9. **Saudi Agricultural Bank,** Riyadh, offers cheap finance to Saudi farmers.
10. **Saudi Arabian Airlines**—SAUDIA, Jiddah—is the national airline.
11. **Saudi Arabian Monetary Agency,** Riyadh, performs the functions of a central bank.

12. **King Abdul Aziz City for Science and Technology,** Riyadh (KAACST).

13. **Saudi Arabian Standards Organisation,** Riyadh.

14. **Saudi Basic Industries Corporation,** Riyadh, was set up so as to enter into joint ventures with foreign companies for the establishment of major industries in Saudi Arabia.

15. **Saudi Hotels and Resort Co. (Sharco),** Riyadh, finances new hotels and other projects to develop tourism/recreation facilities.

16. **Saudi Consulting House,** Riyadh, provides guidelines for private investment in manufacturing operations.

17. **Saudi Development Fund,** Riyadh, makes loans on non-commercial terms to governments of developing countries.

18. **Saudi Industrial Development Fund,** Riyadh, provides 50 per cent cheap finance for manufacturing industry.

19. **Saudi Ports Authority,** Riyadh.

Further details are available from the Department of Trade and Industry, Overseas Trade Division 4, Saudi Arabia Desk. Tel: (071) 215 5052/4362.

5
Customs and Courtesies

The way of life in Saudi Arabia, and indeed, throughout the Muslim world, is such a contrast for most Westerners that it is difficult to know where to start an explanation of it. Saudis are an extremely cultivated people with an ancient and glorious heritage. If you slow down, adapt to their culture, and are as hospitable as they are, you will find living in Saudi Arabia, or any other Muslim country, to be a rich experience.

A returned expatriate offers the following insights:

Nothing is going to be the same—virtually nothing. Don't expect it or, for that matter, don't even want it to be a duplicate of your own country. Although it is hard for some of us, the essential point is this: you do the adapting. They are not going to adapt to us; why should they? The Westerner who can relax and be tolerant of difference will get along with minimum stress.

Along with patience and tolerance, another vital ingredient for success in Saudi Arabia in ingenuity. We are used to more supportive services than we realise: tourist offices, traveller's aids, information desks, research librarians, telephone answering services . . . In Saudi Arabia, what you do not work out for yourself will not get done. You solve your own problems—and in an alien language.

Saudis are in a period of great transition, and the last thing they want are lectures about progress. They can see for themselves exactly what they want from the West, and they also can see with equal clarity what they want to reject. Some of our ways disturb them, and they are quite aware of the results of Western permissiveness.

A common Western stereotype about all Arabs is that 'you

cannot trust them.' This is a mistake. Bear in mind that in Saudi Arabia everyone knows everyone else, and secrets or unlawful pursuits are difficult to hide. As a result, there is a high level of integrity. One should assume that people will be honest, rather than the reverse.

Other general assumptions can be made about Saudis, although there are always exceptions to any generality. Saudis are anxious to do well by people: most are very friendly and have a quick, lively sense of humour. They offer hospitality quicky and sincerely, and they practise their religious beliefs faithfully.

Some foreigners are put off by the paradoxes they find until they realise that the country operates on a double standard or a perceptual duality that divides the world into two parts: age/youth, men/women, foreigners/Saudis, Arab/non-Arab, Muslim/non-Muslin. For example, Saudis may expect you as a Westerner to be on time, even if they are not themselves.

VALUES

Dignity and respect

Two values Saudis hold most dear are those of respect and dignity. The degree to which visibly demonstrated respect enters into daily relationships is one of the most striking things about Saudi culture and Islamic culture generally.

All people are treated respectfully, from the beggar on the street to co-workers to supervisors. Arab proverbs emphasise their deep-felt sense of true equality: 'Men are not measured by the bushel!' and 'Credit goes to the seamstress not to the needle.' This does not mean that you should kowtow: it means that everyone is due visible, expressed respect without regard to rank. It means you consciously extend recognition to every porter, waiter, taxi driver, or shopkeeper. Look them in the face; smile; speak to them. It is remarkable how many of us overlook such people, as if they were invisible, however democratic and friendly we may otherwise be.

In the Arab world it is particularly important to show respect to a person with whom you are meeting or socialising. For example, everyone usually rises when a guest enters; you should do so too. Then shake hands with the newcomer. You will also want to rise to show respect for older people or people of higher rank. You can demonstrate respect by greeting senior guests at the door of their car with the same courtesy again extended on their departure. If an Arab insists that you stay comfortably in your living room and not come out, interpret this as merely a formality and ignore it. Go to the gate with him and wish him Godspeed (in Arabic if you can).

Other ways to show your regard for a person are to avoid any words or gestures that indicate that you are pressed for time, such as sneaking a look at your watch. End a conversation gradually, never abruptly, no matter how busy you feel, lest you give the impression of dismissing your visitor. Be generous with bows and smiles and courteous gestures, such as holding doors open and the like.

As mentioned before, anger, hot words and curses are offensive and should be avoided completely. Words, good or bad, have great power in the Arab culture. Politeness, tact, forbearance, patience and understanding are vital, no matter how hard they are to maintain. These qualities communicate respect for others and a sense of one's own dignity.

Names and terms of address

The Arab notion of what constitutes a name is often confusing to a newcomer. The word **ibn** (son of) is commonly used in names, and several generations may be added, for example, Hassan ibn Uthman ibn Abdullah ibn Nasri. As a result, it is not considered necessary to use a family name, but rather a person's first name, with titles before it to show respect: for example, 'Dr Ahmad' or 'Professor Salim'.

Those who will be doing much business with government officials may find it useful to talk with the protocol officer at their embassy when they arrive for helpful advice about both royal and governmental protocol regarding terms of address. For example, when adddressing a minister who is of the royal family (and there are said to be several thousand princes), you should say 'Your Royal Highness' or at least 'Your Highness' depending on what others do. If the minister is not royalty, 'Your Excellency' is the correct title to use.

Introductions and greetings

Introductions are carried out much as they are in Western societies. The name of the highest-ranking person is mentioned first, as in 'Your Excellency, I'd like to introduce you to Mr John Smith. Mr Smith, this is His Excellency . . .' Whether or not you have been introduced to everyone in a room or an office, treat them as if you have. The fact that you are all there under the host's roof means, by your very presence, that you are all part of his circle.

Saudi greetings often pose a problem for Westerners, especially Americans, who often greet an entire roomful of people with a general 'hello everyone'. The Saudi greets everyone in the room separately, shakes hands, and goes through a rather lengthy sequence of ritualised greetings. The handshaking is continued until the greeting is complete. The handshake in itself carries meaning. Instead of using a strong grip, shake gently, almost limply. If at all possible, learn the most common greeting phrases and replies in Arabic before you go to Saudi Arabia. Knowing even just that much Arabic will put you at a distinct advantage in developing the personal relationship that is so vital to doing business with Saudis.

Hospitality
The entire system of Arab hospitality is based on a delicate balance of mutual obligations. This means, in essence, that an invitation must be returned, that a gift deserves a reciprocal and more or less equal gift, and that friendly and gracious gestures should be accepted and returned. The goal is for both parties to express their hospitality and generosity but for neither to end up feeling overobligated. Hospitality is paramount among Saudi values, originating from life in the desert. Visitors were rare, and anyone who came to your tent, even an enemy, was both protected and made welcome. Lifestyle has changed dramatically since those days, but the custom has not.

You will be offered coffee, tea or soft drinks all day long and on all kinds of occasions—during a visit to a man's office or on entering a shop, for example. The offering and acceptance of a beverage is a ritual that has symbolic importance, and you cannot refuse. To do so is considered rude. When calling on someone, stay until a beverage has been served. You should follow the same procedure with your guests—never fail to offer a beverage to a visitor, business or social, however brief the call, and if there is more than one, serve in order of rank.

The cups or glasses in which the beverage is served are very small (usually without handles) and filled only about a quarter full. Whether you want it or not, finish the first serving and at least sip at the second. After you have been served three times, hold out your cup, rocking it gently from side to side as an indication that you want no more, turn the cup upside down or put your hand over it. A verbal 'no thank you' will probably not be sufficient. You must show you wish no more by your actions as well.

Tea in Saudi Arabia is very sweet, sometimes brewed with mint. Coffee is normally green or yellow, and it has quite a different flavour from what you may be accustomed to. Cardamom seeds, cloves or saffron are often added. Coffee is usually served in a brass or copper pot with a long spout which is stuffed with straw or fibre to strain the liquid (different from Turkish coffee with its thick grounds).

Smoking is restricted in certain instances. For example, it is customary not to smoke before any member of the royal family nor in the streets of Riyadh (since it is the capital) nor anywhere in public during Ramadan. In a Saudi home, refrain from smoking unless your host does so first. In fact, you would do well to keep smoking to a minimum outside your own home.

If you visit a Saudi home, you will be received and treated with utmost care, no matter how busy or how inconvenienced your host. Since your host would never be so impolite as to mention by word or attitude that you have offended him, we offer a few rules for visiting in a Saudi home.

Saudis love lively conversation and particularly enjoy compliments about the country, the local soccer matches, or anything you admire. There are, however, a few subjects to avoid—family affairs are considered private matters, and your host neither wants to tell you about his family nor hear about yours. This restriction is particularly hard for Westerners who love to talk about family activities and their children's accomplishments.

It is also wise to avoid discussion of religion and politics unless you know your hosts quite well. However, when you do talk about politics, most Saudis are enthusiastic speakers. They now feel part of the wider Arab world and are no longer as isolated as they were in the past, even though news is still censored to some degree.

Saudis don't visit each other during siesta time (1400–1600 hours, i.e., 2:00–4:00 pm) nor does one drop in unexpectedly at other times. Muslims remove their shoes on entering a home, and guests should follow suit. When dining on the floor, tuck your legs under you so the soles of your feet are hidden. Watch how others are doing it. As you have probably heard before, showing the soles of your shoes or sandals to an Arab's face is a serious insult. If you are sitting opposite an Arab in a comfortable chair, be sure that your legs are not crossed in such a way that your soles are pointed toward him. In fact, never put your feet up on a stool, desk, train seat, or any other raised surface.

If you openly admire a specific object in the home of an Arab, the object may be given to you then and there or even delivered later to your hotel or home. As you can imagine, this is extremely embarrassing. If you try to return the gift, you risk seriously hurting your host's feelings. This custom is slowly changing, but it is still best not to admire specific items belonging to another— rings, vases, pictures or anything else. It is fine, however, to express general admiration or praise for a beautiful room, a magnificent collection of carpets or lovely fountains.

Separation of men and women

Traditional Arab custom requires almost total separation of men and women outside their own homes. If a Saudi issues an invitation, wives will often be excluded. Foreign men should be careful not to speak of Arab women unless they have been introduced, and even then, inquiring about an Arab's wife is considered inappropriate. You must never photograph an Arab woman without permission from her husband. In fact, it is best not to photograph an Arab woman under any circumstances.

Because of increasing conservatism in the Kingdom, it is difficult for foreign women to meet Saudi women. However, some foreign women find ways to work with their Saudi counterparts in hospitals, girls' schools or elsewhere, and some of the more modern Saudi men allow their wives to meet with foreign women now and then, so long as the foreigners abide by the strict rules of procedure regarding dress and behaviour. A useful point of contact for British women before going to Saudi Arabia might be a local Muslim Ladies' Circle, which is usually attached to a mosque, university, or college. Some of the educational/cultural organisations listed in 'Useful Addresses' might also be able to help in this regard. By and large, however, foreign women must be content to mix with other foreigners. There are many coffee mornings, teas and women's parties as well as other more substantial activities within the foreign compounds (see chapter 9 for more information).

Hotels and restaurants generally have 'family rooms', where women and children are served. Sometimes sections are set aside where men may eat with their families, but in public Arab men generally eat in areas reserved for them alone.

The mutawwa'een (religious police)

The job of the **mutawwa'een** is to enforce the observance of Islamic practices and moral standards in the community. They are appointed by a religious society known as the Society for the Propagation of Virtue and Suppression of Vice, which is sponsored by the government and supervised by the king and the ulema. Mutawwa'een are invariably pious, righteous and conservative men. To be appointed a mutawwa, one must apply to the Society and pass a test on religious knowledge.

Mutawwa'een are expected to correct (and if necessary, report) infractions of rules; in many cases they can make arrests or designate punishment. They may, for example, do any of the following:

1. use a switch on a woman whose clothing improperly reveals her arms or legs;
2. force a man to undergo a public haircut;
3. require women to leave public areas, such as an outdoor café;
4. enter offices to ensure that no women are working there illegally or are improperly sharing office space with men;
5. admonish Muslims who are not praying at appointed times;
6. enforce the abstinence from food, drink and tobacco during Ramadan (in fact, they are much more visible and strict at this time of year);
7. report the possession or consumption of alcohol or drugs; and
8. even ask couples in public places whether they are married.

Mutawwa'een are also responsible for enforcing the law that requires business establishments to close for prayer: thus, they can compel customers to leave or force businessmen to close their doors during prayer time.

Before you begin thinking of the Mutawwa'een as a Saudi version of secret police, however, let us assure you that they are not out to frighten or intimidate people, nor do they seek out foreigners or try to humiliate anyone personally. You need not fear them if your behaviour is correct.

SOCIAL OCCASIONS

Saudi parties

If you are invited to a Saudi home for a party (which invariably includes a meal), by all means go. Conversation will be spirited, witty and interesting, and the food delicious.

A normal Arab meal usually consists of rice, often flavoured with raisins and almonds, served with roast lamb, savoury sauces, and fruits. Your host will be delighted if you take second helpings. If you are not provided with eating implements, you will find it easiest to form the rice into small balls, dip them into the sauces, and then eat them. The bread may also prove helpful for picking up food. In urban homes you are likely to be served bowls of tomatoes, beans, carrots or potatoes, which may have been canned or frozen, and you will probably be seated at a table set with familiar tableware. Your host will be honoured if you try at least a small amount of everything offered. Indeed, so many dishes may be served that you might wish to limit yourself to small portions of each to avoid overeating.

At the end of the meal, coffee will be served; the wafting of incense will then let you know that the party is over. The guest says **shukran** (thank you) and the host answers with **fi aman allah** (go in the care of God). You should learn to use both of these phrases so you can use the latter with guests who are leaving your home or office.

If you should be invited to an Arab feast, rejoice; it is a great experience. It may be a traditional meal served on mats or carpets around which guests are seated on the floor (with their feet under them), or it may be a dinner party just like those in other parts of the world. If you eat on the floor, put your left hand behind you. We have mentioned elsewhere that in Islam the left hand is used for private bodily functions. Therefore, it is never extended to another person when giving or receiving food (or for that matter, gifts, documents, money or anything else).

If the group is large, a small camel may be the mainstay of the meal, or perhaps a sheep or goat. The meat will probably be boiled or roasted whole and served with buttered, steaming rice on copper or brass trays from which you serve yourself. You will tear off chunks of meat and bread, which you then use to scoop chicken, fruits, vegetables, pastries and sweets from side dishes (watch what others do). The sequence of foods and flavours may be new to you.

Do not be surprised if the host remains standing and does not eat at all: his concern for his guests' comfort is paramount.

When a guest is finished, he says **alhamdulillah** (thanks be to God), leans back and rises. Soap and towels will be provided for the washing of hands, after which rose water and cologne may be poured over them. After-dinner coffee is served, and then incense may be passed to be inhaled and wafted into one's clothes and beard (again, the pleasure in fragrance). After the incense, as we mentioned earlier, it is time to depart; do not try to sit and converse.

International social functions
Under current circumstances most social life among expatriates takes place in the compounds. Entertaining there follows the normal social customs of other parts of the world, except that there is no alcohol. You can expect, though, to be invited to (or to give) parties outside the compound. For example, you will probably meet people on embassy staffs and in other international business organisations and through them may be invited to various affairs. All written invitations should be answered promptly, in the language in which they are extended if at all possible. Saudis usually do not respond to 'RSVP' on invitations, but you should continue to do so. Send a thank-you note, too, even if your Saudi guests do not. The Saudis will expect you to honour the code of etiquette from your own culture. If you do not, you will be suspect. 'Casual dress' on an embassy invitation generally means a sports jacket but usually no tie (to be on the safe side, you might want to bring one in your pocket). Women should follow the usual public dress code: a midcalf-length dress with sleeves and a high neckline unless otherwise specified. 'Informal' usually means suit and tie for men, Sunday best for ladies. 'Formal' means dinner jacket for men (if you have one; otherwise, a dark suit) and long gowns for women.

When given at the large hotels, parties can become extremely lavish and expensive, but such extravagance is not necessary. Plan your own party any way you like, especially when entertaining the international community (as distinct from the Arab community). If Saudis are present, however, they should always be served before either host or hostess. Guests come first in this hospitable land.

Whatever you serve, be sure there is plenty of it. Take trouble over your dishes and spread ample buffets. A sense of bounty—plenty and more than plenty—is a mark of hospitality. Never serve pork in any form when Arabs are present. Muslims are forbidden to eat it and do not even like to see or smell it.

It is interesting to note that the more formal a party is, the shorter the pre-dinner conversation and the earlier the departure. Official dinners can be as short as an hour or so. It is obvious why it is so important to be prompt. (For more information, we suggest you read the following chapters in *Understanding Arabs* by Margaret Nydell: 'Men and Women', 'Social formalities and Etiquette', and 'The Arabic language'; see Further Reading.)

6
Household Pointers

HOUSING

In the 1970s housing in Saudi Arabia was in short supply and very expensive. But times have changed and the major cities are heavily overbuilt. Consequently, finding very nice housing at reasonable rents is no longer a problem. Large firms are required to provide housing for their foreign employees, and some landlords lease their apartment compounds specifically to expatriates. Unfortunately, even though plentiful housing exists, it is very difficult for individuals to find it on their own. You should be sure that your company plans to help you locate suitable living quarters. Real estate brokers tend to be unreliable, try to charge too much money, and, if their fee is paid in advance, often come up empty-handed. Rent is usually payable for as much as a year in advance. If you rent an individual villa, you may want to sign a maintenance agreement, which includes plumbing, electricity, air-conditioning and structural repairs. Do not pay this in advance; if you do, nothing will be fixed or maintained.

Compounds built by large companies often look like Western suburban neighbourhoods, with villas made of gypsum, stucco or even marble. Many in the Eastern Province were built in the 1950s and 1960s by ARAMCO and other large companies. These homes are primarily one-storey, cement-block structures with grassy yards, pine and oleander, fuchsia, and bougainvillea. 'It is Pasadena to a "T",' said one American returning from Dhahran. Some of the newer villas have central air-conditioning, but be wary. Air conditioners have a relatively short life in Saudi Arabia, and the cost of running them is quite high. It is more practical, though a great deal noisier, to have separate units in each room.

Rapid expansion creates its own problems, no matter where it

takes place, and Saudi Arabia is no exception. Housing developments are often completed before basic services such as water
mains, sewers and telephones are connected, and the wait for these
utilities can be as long as six months. Having a telephone installed
is particularly troublesome. The demand far exceeds the supply,
and again, the wait may be a long one. If you are looking for housing
for yourself or for your staff, keep these points in mind and look
for compounds a year or so old.

Utilities

Water

The main cities now have water piped to all but the newest
neighbourhoods. Some of the older homes in neighbourhoods like
Malaz in Riyadh still have cisterns which must be filled by water
trucks. If you have rented a house with a cistern, the landlord needs
to sign up for water service (quite expensive), and you should
discuss this before signing the lease. Having the tank cleaned at
regular intervals is very important.

Do not be startled if your hot water runs cold at first, or the
cold, hot. Sometimes the cold water—coming from the tank on the
roof—is hot; the hot water—sitting in a tank in the bathroom where
it is relatively cool—may in fact be cooler.

Electricity

Although electric current is basically 110 volts, 60 Hertz AC, many
houses are built with both 110 and 220 wiring to outlets—which
all look the same. The new tenant should test and label each outlet
(with an AC tester) to avoid plugging the wrong appliance into the
wrong socket. Since both Hertz and voltages vary even from house
to house, it is a wise idea to pack a few all-purpose adapters in
your suitcases to protect your small appliances from current
fluctuations. Small travelling converters come in two sizes: 50-watt
adapters, which are useful for electric shavers, calculators, and the
like; and 1,600-watt adapters, which are useful for toasters and
other small appliances. The biggest advantage of adapters is their
small size and the fact that they change both voltage levels and
Hertz.

Transformers, on the other hand, change only voltage levels, not
frequencies. Transformers come in various sizes, ranging from 50
watts (about 1–2 pounds) to 2,500 watts (35 pounds). 'Step down'

transformers will allow American appliances to be used on 220-volt electrical systems while the 'step up' transformers will allow European appliances to be used on 110-volt lines. The way to know what size to buy is to add up the wattage (or amperage) of the appliances that will be attached to that transformer. You will find this wattage listed with the serial number on each appliance nameplate. Your transformer should handle about 20 per cent above this total wattage to allow for the extra start-up power needed. For example, if your coffee pot takes 800 watts, you will need a 1,000-watt transformer. Most expatriates have a number of transformers at various outlets throughout the house.

There are various electrical firms that advertise international servicing; of course, they can supply necessary parts as well. Understandably, your warranty is no longer valid once you alter an appliance. Remember, though, you cannot change clocks, film projectors or motors that have to adapt to various speeds (like blenders). This is why it is better to buy these items in the Kingdom.

Be especially careful about connecting or disconnecting appliances because cables are not always earthed. If you have wet hands, are standing in a puddle, or resting against a nearby pipe or tap, you are a conductor. Outlet covers are an especially good idea if you have children of crawling age who could put wet fingers into sockets.

Power shutdowns used to be quite common. The power system throughout the country is now able to meet the demand, but as in any country, power failures occur and contingency plans should be made. In the case of a shutdown, turn everything off except your refrigerator and freezer—both to avoid damage and, even more important, to lessen the power surge when service is resumed. If there is warning of a long shutdown, stuff all the empty spaces in your freezer and refrigerator with newspaper to conserve the cold temperature. Also, put blankets or an old quilt over the freezer to insulate it from the outside, but be careful not to cover the cooling mechanism and motor.

As a precaution, keep handy a supply of candles, a paraffin lamp and plenty of flashlights for power cuts. If shutdowns occur frequently in the area where you live, you would be wise to acquire the habit of turning off and unplugging heating and cooking appliances when they are not in use, especially if you are leaving the house for a long time. Otherwise, the stoppage, followed by a power surge, can damage appliances or even cause a fire.

If you have any other electrical problems or queries, you can contact the Institution of Electrical Engineers' representative in Saudi Arabia: Dr Mohamed N. Khayata, BSc(Eng), PhD, FIEE, at the Saudi Fund for Development, PO Box 50483, Riyadh.

Gas
Bottled gas is widely used for both cooking and heating. The cylinders must be stored outside the house and an extra tank or two kept on hand lest shortages occur. Check connecting rubber hoses from time to time, and always be certain that ventilation is adequate.

HOUSEHOLD HELP

Because of the influx of foreigners and the expulsion of many immigrant workers, there is a shortage of household help. All available help will, for the most part, be men—though never Saudis, who do not do housework. Slavery was lawful in Saudi Arabia until 1962, and slaves were mostly African. While no colour discrimination resulted from slavery, a lasting distaste for housework did. Houseboys—or menservants—are likely to come from the Sudan, Yemen, or Gaza (Palestinian). Many people recommend the Sudanese as especially pleasant and reliable. Other male servants come from Somalia, India, Pakistan, Bangladesh and the Philippines. Women servants are generally hired for child care and may be Egyptian or Ethiopian. Although domestics often understand a bit of English, hardly any can speak much of it.

Hiring and paying household help
Since there is considerable turnover among servants in the international community as families move on to new assignments, the usual way to find help is by word of mouth—there are no employment agencies. When you interview someone, take a good interpreter with you. Investigate potential household help with great care. In many cases you will be responsible for the person's medical care, food, clothing, living accommodation, visa, contract, and tickets back and forth to his own country. Find out as much as possible before you take on those responsibilities. The matter of hiring and managing help is complex, and often expatriates are not prepared for the issues and problems that arise.

When you take on a new servant, be sure that he or she knows you are starting on a trial basis. Work out what you will do about food—some employers provide it, others prefer to give an allowance and let the help buy their own. Also, clarify the living arrangements. Servants' quarters are provided in virtually all houses and apartments. Many servants live in, especially women, but some come only for the day.

Be sure arrangements regarding wages are worked out beforehand also. Naturally, if you must train a servant first, the wages should be lower than if he or she is already accustomed to working for Westerners.

As was mentioned earlier, no expatriates of any nationality are covered by GOSI, the national insurance plan, but you must be sure your help's papers and documents are all in order. Check the status of their passports, visas and work permits before you hire. If you do not, you may be liable to heavy fines. Yes, you are responsible, not your servant. Check carefully with local authorities about these details. Westerners already in Saudi Arabia can offer assistance as can your own embassy or consulate, or the Ministry of Labour.

If servants live with you, you will be responsible for providing clothing and food, and you will want to give an occasional present like a transistor radio. Understandably, the wages will be lower than if they buy their own clothes and food and live separately. They will expect a gift each time you return from vacation and will be crushed if you forget them.

Rises are customarily given once a year. You are also expected to give approximately one month's wages as a bonus once a year during the Ramadan–Hajj holidays.

Plan to give your help at least two half-days or one full day off a week, preferably Friday, as that is the Muslim religious day. Since they generally do not have their families with them, be reasonably generous about time off for home visits. It is acceptable, though, to insist that your help take home leave during the time that you are away the longest. Many will also want time off for the Hajj each year. Christians often take time off at Easter. As is true throughout the society, domestic help work very, very slowly during Ramadan. If you accept that fact beforehand, it will save you frustration later.

Be sure to require a full physical examination at the time of hiring, including a chest x-ray, blood tests for VD and AIDS, and then watch cleanliness procedures to ensure that health standards are maintained. You will want to provide supplies that will help servants keep their clothes and hands clean, especially those who handle food. Finally, be sure immunisations are kept up to date.

Attitude toward your household help
Do not expect your help to know exactly what you want. You must be patient and teach them by working alongside them for a while. They may not be familiar with electrical equipment, so be sure to teach them safety rules for using eletricity as well as operating instructions.

Most expatriates who are not accustomed to having servants are understandably nervous about it. As one expatriate wife explained it,

> To me the greatest concern when coming out here was how I would get on with the help—and they with me. Some pointers that I have learned may help other people be more relaxed. First, assume that the servants are trustworthy and willing to please. Be patient with them. If Arabic is hard for you, think how hard English is for them. Stealing is very rare in Saudi Arabia, so by all means trust your help, and let them know that you do. Compliment them readily and often.

Your houseboy should be treated with full respect by all members of the family. Children should be taught to listen to him as if he were an uncle. Never let the children laugh at him when, for example, he eats with his fingers. Some parents are concerned lest their children be spoiled by having household help. One family handled this potential problem by making it clear from the start that the help were there for the adults; children still had to make their own beds and tidy their own rooms.

Part of showing respect is honouring your servants' dignity. Show them how you want something done or correct what you feel they are doing wrong, but do so in private—never in front of others. Tell them calmly and clearly what it is you want, but express no anger.

Household duties
The average work schedule for household help is 0700–1200 and 1500–1800, Saturday to Thursday. Evening work should be by special arrangement, with separate compensation.

Before you hire help, be clear in your own mind how you feel about them having guests. If they live in, your house becomes their home, and they need to have some place where they can entertain family or friends during their time off, which may mean several noisy people all at once. Give this matter considerable thought and then state your policy very clearly to your live-in help.

There are no hard and fast guidelines about servants' duties, but they are more or less as follows:

Drivers

Since women are not allowed to drive, drivers are often essential. Usually they do not live in, and they expect extra payment if they work very late at night. In addition to their driving duties, they are expected to do routine maintenance on your car. If your driver does live in, he will often be prepared to take care of the garden, maintain the pool and wash the car. A driver must, of course, have a Saudi driver's licence, and you will probably want to purchase substantial insurance for him. Check with other expatriates about this matter of insurance.

Cooks

Usually the cook is the most important servant since he is the most skilled, in addition to cooking, he shops, plans menus if you wish, and sometimes also serves the meals. Your cook can teach you many things about location and availability of food items. After you get to know each other, do the marketing together until you become acquainted with local prices. Then work out a budget and let him market for you. Keep in mind, however, that marketing, especially in the souqs, is one way to make a connection with the Saudi culture. Think carefully before you turn over all marketing responsibilities to your cook.

Houseboys and maids

Houseboys do the house-cleaning, laundry, serving, and may help run the kitchen. Maids do similar jobs but usually live in and help with children (see chapter 9 for more details about children). In the desert world, house-cleaning is vital because of the constant assault of sand and dust. After a sandstorm, you will be glad that you have household help. **Shammals** or dust storms blow for several days, and since dust harbours disease, cleaning up afterwards is essential.

Gardeners
Gardeners may be full or part-time employees and often come with the house. In some cases, you will pay them directly; in others, the landlord may take care of the wages. Discuss the question with your landlord and be sure that one, but not both, of you is paying them. (The gardeners prefer to be paid by the Western employer because that way they can be sure they will be paid on time.) In addition to their gardening duties, which include a great deal of watering in the desert climate, gardeners will also wash windows and do other outdoor jobs.

Guards or gateboys
Guards answer the gate and keep out peddlers, beggars, small boys who run wild in Saudi Arabia, and animals. The driver or the gardener often handles this job, but if you have neither, you may want to consider having a security man.

BARGAINING AND SHOPPING

Bargaining
On the whole, Saudi Arabia is a society that likes, and expects, to bargain in making a sale, especially in the souqs. Bargaining is part of life and Saudis enjoy it; in fact, they will feel disappointed and hurt if you do not play the game. If you are buying something from the souq that you do not need urgently—a carpet, an old Bedouin chest, some brassware, or whatever—do not be afraid to let the bargaining stretch through two or three weeks, but if you do, be sure to return every two or three days to give your absolute last price and to get his.

One woman who lived in Saudi Arabia for some years gives this advice:

> If a merchant has a carpet for which he is asking 10,000 SR, offer 4000 or 5000. If you bargain well, you may be able to get it for 6000 or 6500. You should raise your price in 50- to 100-riyal blocks; he will very likely lower his in blocks of 500 to 1000. The thing to do is to return to the same merchants on a regular basis. They are delightful people who will get to know you and will appreciate your loyalty. Soon they will begin saving trinkets they think you would like.

As a rough rule of thumb, offer about half of the asking price, then come up to about two-thirds. Do not insult a merchant by starting too low. Naturally, there are no hard and fast rules, but these guidelines give you a starting-point. Make a game of bargaining, and above all, keep your sense of humour and be a good sport. Leave with a pleasant goodbye and a smile, whether you agreed on a price or not.

Shopping

Shopping in Saudi Arabia can either be fast and efficient or a leisurely adventure. While new buildings of glass and steel are the order of the day, there is enough left of the old world to please the romantics among us. Vegetable souqs sell everything from dates to eggs. The women's souq, smelling of both cheap and expensive perfumes, is an enticing, magical place. The wonderful fragrance of incense and spices wafts through the carpet souqs, and the scent of sandalwood permeates the **shesha** (water-pipe) alleys. Most dazzling of all are the gold souqs. The alleys of small shops selling eighteen, twenty-one and twenty-four carat gold and sterling silver are always thronged with women, local and foreign. Styles of jewellery range from chic Italian designs to gold bibs and belts that are favoured as dowry items by Bedouin women.

In the souqs you can shop for luggage, pots and pans, clocks, watches, radios, cassette players, carpets, tents, freshly-ground flour, fresh coffee, tools, fencing materials, spare parts for cars, cassette tapes, tailor-made clothes, and almost anything else under the sun. There are also souqs selling brass, antiques and old (Roman) coins, and a falcon souq on Thursdays in Justice Square in Riyadh. The maze of alleys goes in all directions, and you can get lost very easily. Carefully note where you leave your car and constantly be thinking of where you are and how you will return. In other words, develop your navigational skills in the souq before you get seriously lost. During your strolls notice the scribes who write letters for those who cannot read. Nowadays scribes use typewriters (Arabic of course), not pens. In the oldest parts of the souqs you will see earthenware water jars suspended upside down in their stands (much like a Western water cooler), with a tin cup on a chain ready for thirsty shoppers to help themselves to a drink. Needless to say, you probably will not want to quench your thirst from these jars.

In all the major cities there are now hardware chains just like those in the United Kingdom. Large, well-stocked stationery stores carry complete supplies or artists' and drafting materials and a limited number of popular books. Toy shops in the Kingdom are now second to none. As you might expect, you do not bargain for prices in modern stores or supermarkets. These stores have fixed prices, and you can maintain a charge account if you wish.

Supermarkets
Supermarkets are now everywhere. They are similar to British hypermarkets, and they stock both local foods and goods and fruit from all over the world. Local foods are very good and far less expensive than the imported equivalents. Nevertheless, you will enjoy the wide range of international products. Caviar, for example, sells for £1 a jar. You may not find your favourite brands, but you will most likely find a substitute. Fresh, frozen and canned foods and even TV dinners are all available at a high price, but the supply fluctuates. There are also many wonderful, exotic herbs and spices available, and an adventurous cook can have a wonderful time learning and experimenting with new tastes, flavours and foods. The only spices you cannot find are cream of tartar, poppy seeds and nutmeg. (You will not find extracts which contain alcohol, such as vanilla. You can, of course, buy imitation vanilla.) You will find a wide variety of cleaning items (SOS, Comet, Ajax) as well as the usual array of dish racks, Teflon pots, blenders, pressure cookers, and so forth. You do need to take a good supply of airtight containers and/or Ziploc bags. Cubed ice, safe to use in drinks, can be bought at all major supermarkets, and there are ice factories in many cities and towns.

The main supermarkets are Tamimi and Fouad (originally Safeway), Al Azizia (originally A&P), and Panda. Euromarche, from France, has large stores in locations throughout Riyadh. Al Azizia was established by Prince Talal, a brother of the king, and 25 per cent of the profits are donated to UNESCO.

When you see items you want, buy them immediately, for you may not see them the next time you look. Between shipments of imported goods, some items become scarce or unavailable. For example, if you use marshmallow crème for Christmas sweets buy it as soon as it appears on the shelves in July or August. By the holidays it will be all gone. When you go to the market in the summertime, take a thermal bag or a picnic cooler to bring home frozen goods and fresh meat. With air-conditioned vehicles spoilage is not such a problem, but a cooler is still a wise precaution. The best time of the day to shop, particularly in the summer, is in the morning or after sundown when it is less crowded and cooler.

Supermarkets close for a half hour for each prayer time and two hours on Friday so employees can go to the mosque. Other shops usually close at noon prayer and do not open until after mid-afternoon prayer, closing again for sunset and evening prayers. This means planning shopping trips carefully between prayer times; otherwise, you are standing on the pavement or sitting in your car for half an hour. If you are in a supermarket at prayer time, you may stay and continue shopping, but you cannot check out until it reopens. Failure by a Westerner to observe prayer time can cause problems (arrest, fines, caning) for both the Westerner and the shopkeeper.

KITCHEN ADVICE

Kitchen hygiene
Kitchen cleanliness is vitally important, and a few simple precautions make a lot of difference in avoiding illness. Personal cleanliness is essential, including not only washing but drying hands before handling food. Teach your help to use only clean towels and to keep kitchen towels absolutely separate from their personal linen. Also, drying the dishes as well as washing them in hot water helps protect you from amoebic dysentery. Most villas have dishwashers, but servants do not like to use them. Spend as much time as you need to teach them how to use the dishwasher and then insist that they do so.

Meat, eggs and milk
Most Westerners buy imported meat, either fresh or frozen, from the United States and Australia. It is packaged in cuts that are familiar to Westerners and does not require any special treatment. If you buy local meat, however, you need to let it age before you eat it. First, wash and dry it thoroughly and carefully (germs thrive in moisture), then sprinkle it with a meat tenderiser, and finally, put it into the refrigerator for a few days. You can certainly freeze meat, but remember that it will not age in the freezer—it will thaw out just the way you put it in. Meat frozen for seventeen days will be free of parasites or their eggs. If you cannot freeze your meat, then cook it thoroughly, preferably in a pressure cooker.

Fresh fish is available daily in the markets of seaports, such as Jiddah and Al Khobar. Go early in the morning for the freshest seafood and best selection. Fish is transported to Riyadh by refrigerated trucks two or three times a week.

Chicken farms abound to the point of overproduction. Poultry products are exported by the Kingdom, and prices are now accordingly quite low. Eggs are available and mostly fresh, but you can save yourself problems if you check them carefully. If you buy your eggs at the souq, ask the merchant to place the eggs in a bowl of water. Any eggs that float are spoiled. At home, break each egg separately into a bowl to check for freshness before you toss it into the other ingredients. Eggs come (courtesy of nature) with a protective, though invisible, film. Leave it on while they are in the refrigerator, but when you are ready to use the eggs, be sure to wash them carefully even if they don't look dirty. If you buy eggs from a supermarket and find they are not 'up to snuff', you can return them and have them replaced. Here again, the water test will give you a good initial indication.

Modern dairies supply fresh milk, buttermilk, sour cream, cottage cheese, and yoghurt to the supermarkets. Dairy products are also imported from Denmark, Australia, Holland, the United States and elsewhere. Good powdered baby-formula and several well-known prepared brands are available, as are baby bottles and other products for infants.

HOW HARD IS IT REALLY? REPLIES FROM WOMEN

One expatriate woman says:

> Not being allowed to drive is hard at first. We are all so accustomed to jumping into a car and taking off, but you get used to it. Many companies provide transportation for their people. Taxis are plentiful, and public buses are available too. You must use the women's section, of course, even if you and your husband or son have to separate. But the buses are good, reliable, and have many routes. There are advantages to having a driver. It is very nice to be able to stop anywhere and jump out of the car without worrying about parking it. Off you go to shop, knowing that the driver will wait as long as you need him.

Women do have to face the loss of much personal freedom. As one wife writes:

> I miss playing golf, going out bowling once in a while, having a drink sometimes with friends, going to the movies, going to the theatre. We can't even have religious services here because it is against Saudi law for non-Muslims to practise publicly.

However, those who live in compounds—be it a community of villas or an apartment building set aside for foreigners—find most of them comfortable and attractive. Most supply a wide range of sports facilities and entertainment, including children's programmes; and, of course, there are swimming-pools. Some even include golf courses and bowling alleys. Weekly trips are often organised to various parts of town. The situation encourages a great deal of neighbourliness and friendliness, and the compound becomes almost an extended family for many expatriates. Children usually roam freely within the compounds. Another expatriate wife has wise advice:

> Depending on their company, foreigners are likely to have substantial compensations that they should not forget when they are tempted to complain about restrictions: free housing and utilities, free schooling for the children, high salaries, free transportation for the family, and travel holidays—sometimes several—each year for 'rest and recreation', plus a regular annual vacation. Anyone getting that many travel breaks and stashing away those salaries should be able to handle the situation without complaining.

There are many opportunities to do all kinds of things with a wide variety of people. Furthermore, Saudi Arabia is in itself a fascinating place, even if—in public—women do have to take a back seat while they are there. There is still plenty that they can do with friends of many nationalities.

When taking a family to Saudi Arabia, husbands should be aware that they will have to take a much more active role in shopping, taking the children to school, and generally being a chauffeur whenever needed. It is very difficult for women to lose their independence, and husbands will need to help their families even when they feel like coming home after a difficult day at the office, kicking off their shoes and throwing themselves on the couch to relax. If at all possible, hire a driver for the family: it takes the load off everyone.

7
Schools

The Saudi school system follows traditional Muslim teaching methods, that is, learning by rote, and Qur'anic studies constitute a large part of the curriculum. The Saudi government does not encourage non-Muslim children to attend its Muslim schools, and most expatriates prefer that their children continue in a Western-style system so that they will not be left behind when they return home. You will find a range of schools to choose from—all part of the Saudi Arabian government international school system.

By royal decree the government instituted a new international school system in the autumn of 1975, replacing the international school that had existed previously. Divided into British and American sections, it is part of a system which has official support for Western-style education for the approximately 10,000 foreign children in the Kingdom. In accordance with Saudi regulations and local boards of education, school classes are to be divided by sex after the third grade, and no uniforms are required. The ARAMCO School in Dhahran and various schools in Jiddah have become affiliated with this system. The diplomatic quarter in Riyadh has a large branch of the international school dedicated to meeting the needs of the children of diplomats, according to their national standards.

It should also be noted that children educated at these schools in Saudi Arabia do very well when they return to their schools back home. At present there are no high school facilities for foreigners in Saudi Arabia. Families either leave their teenagers at home to finish school or send them to boarding-school in Europe or Bahrain. (Bahrain School, PO Box 116, Jufair Road, Manama, Bahrain.)

The following information regarding some specific schools in Jiddah, Riyadh and the Eastern Province was obtained from the

Royal Embassy of Saudi Arabia in Washington, DC: other information comes from the *International Schools Service Directory of Overseas Schools*, 1990. If the school fees listed below seem high, remember that almost all firms who hire married employees pay the tuition costs for their children. This is over and above salaries and is built into the firm's contract.

JIDDAH

- **The Parents Co-operative School (PCS)** and its **North Campus School**, c/o SAUDIA, PO Box 167, CC 100, Jiddah, Saudi Arabia; kindergarten up to grade nine. PCS and its North Campus branch are owned and operated by Saudia, and both use an American curriculum. Enrolling approximately 2,000 pupils, this excellent school has many extracurricular activities. The school year runs from late August through to early June with winter, spring, and Hajj breaks. To enrol, contact PCS as soon as possible; space fills up quickly. Bring transcripts, report cards and pupil records.

- **Jiddah Preparatory School** has an enrolment of 500 English and Dutch students, pre-kindergarten and up to grade eight. The curriculum follows the British system; Dutch children receive two hours of English language instruction per week. Facilities include a gym, playing-field, swimming-pool and an exceptionally well-stocked library. Bring school records and reports.

- **Continental School**, PO Box 6453, Jiddah 21442, Saudi Arabia; tel: (2) 682-7655; pre-kindergarten to grade twelve. Under the auspices of several embassies, Continental School follows the British curriculum.

- **Manarat Islamic International Schools**, PO Box 2446, Jiddah 21471, Saudi Arabia; tel: (2) 671 9732. These schools cater for English-speaking children of Muslim parents. The curriculum is British and standards are high. There are also French, German, Swedish, Italian, Japanese, Pakistani and Korean schools. Several companies operate schools in their own compounds.

- **Saudi Arabian International School (SAIS)**, c/o Saudi Arabian Airlines, PO Box 167, CC 100, Jiddah, Saudi Arabia; tel: (2) 667 4566; kindergarten and up to grade nine. SAIS of Jiddah enrols approximately 1,000 students, the largest percentage of whom are from the United States. SAIS follows a US curriculum, is well equipped, and offers a wide range of special curricular, extracurricular, and sports activities. Both French and Arabic are taught, and the staff includes a number of specialists for individual students' needs.

RIYADH

Saudi Arabian International School (SAIS).

- **American Section**, PO Box 990, Riyadh 11421, Saudi Arabia; tel: (1) 491 4270; pre-kindergarten through grade nine. The American Section of SAIS is located off the Dhahran road and enrols around, 2,000 pupils. It is well equipped and has facilities for many extracurricular activities. Bring school certificates. Fathers must register children.
- **British Section**, PO Box 2907, Riyadh 11461, Saudi Arabia; tel: (1) 476 3196; ages four to twelve. Located north of Riyadh, the British section of SAIS is also a well-equipped school with a smaller enrolment of 350 pupils. Bring proof of religion, class reports and a birth certificate.
- **French Section**, PO Box 1392, Riyadh 11431, Saudi Arabia; tel: (1) 403 0892. The French section has an enrolment of 400 students. It follows the French curriculum and includes English and Arabic instruction.
    SAIS of Riyadh also includes a German section, a Scandinavian section, and several small company schools in various compounds. There is also a King Khaled International Airport School and several Manarat Schools in Riyadh.

EASTERN PROVINCE: Al Khobar, Dhahran, Dammam

Saudi Arabian International School (SAIS); pre- kindergarten through grade eleven. As with other SAIS schools, this Dhahran District SAIS school is well equipped and well staffed, with a low teacher-student ratio.

- **American Section**, Superintendent, Dhahran Academy, US Consulate General, APO New York 09616; tel: (3) 864 3842. Known as the Dhahran Academy, this section of SAIS is located in the grounds of the US Consulate General.
- **British Section**, PO Box 269, Al Khobar 31411, Saudi

Arabia. The British section accepts only a limited number of students, and the waiting list is often long.

- **French Section**, École Française 2792, Dammam 31461, Saudi Arabia. Catering for 350 students, the French SAIS admits only French-speaking children and follows the Lycée Française curriculum.
- **German Section**. Located in the ALUPCO compound between Al Khobar and Dammam, the German section is quite small—only sixty students or so.
- **Dhahran—Dammam Manarat Schools**. Manarat Schools in Jiddah, tel: (2) 671 9732; Riyadh, tel: (1) 477 8019; London, 29 Belgrave Square, tel: (071) 722 2320.
- **Arabian American Oil Company (ARAMCO) Schools**, Box 73, Dhahran 31311, Saudi Arabia. As might be expected, both staff and student body are predominantly American. Enrolment is approximately 2,000, and teacher—student ratio is low. The curriculum is American, and both French and Arabic are taught, with an impressive variety of special programmes and activities.
- Other branches of SAIS can be found in Jubail, Khamis Mushayt (Northrop tel: (7) 222 2200 ext. 3772), and Taif.
- The address of the Yanbu International School is PO Box 149, Yanbu, Saudi Arabia.

There are many pre-school and play-school groups conducted in private homes in all the major cities and towns. Ask around when you arrive if you are interested.

8
Health and Medical Care

MEDICAL FACILITIES

Medical facilities have improved dramatically in Saudi Arabia in recent years. During the Third Five-Year Plan (1980–5), the Ministry of Health built 320 regional health centres and thirty-six new hospitals. One of the two medical schools which have separate divisions for men and women is in Riyadh, and the second is located in Abha in the Asir region. Other facilities include two medical institutes and five nursing schools. Although the government's goal was to train 15,000 medical personnel by 1988, medical and nursing care is minimal outside government-sponsored, Western-run hospitals. Emergency medical care is available, but except for the large hospitals, it is unreliable (the ambulance service is known as Red Crescent and is not recommended).

Medical care is supposedly free to all Saudi Arabian citizens, but at the best institutions, like the King Faisal Specialist Hospital or the King Khaled Eye Specialist Hospital, the patients are required to pay. The numerous private hospitals are all pay-as-you-go as well. Basically, to say that Saudis have free medical care is stretching the truth somewhat, and one must sympathise when Saudi citizens grumble about all the exceptions to the rule.

Many of the high-quality medical resources that exist are reserved for Saudis and thus are not available to foreigners. Expatriates in Saudi Arabia must therefore have an explicit commitment from their firms that in case of major medical need, they will be flown home at company expense for diagnosis and treatment. Some firms have set up their own medical units for their personnel. The company should at least be able to direct employees to the best local facility.

Most of the hospitals listed below are open to foreigners. A few, labelled 'Saudi only', are not and are included here only for your information.

Riyadh hospitals

- **King Saud Medical Centre** (the University Hospital near Dir'iyah at the north-west corner of the city).
- **King Faisal Specialist Hospital and Research Centre** (in Nassiriyah)—planned by the late King Faisal to be one of the great medical centres of the world. It is an excellent facility, but unfortunately it is available to foreigners only by royal order (a letter from the king). If you arrive at the emergency room near death, they will take care of you, but it is better to go to a hospital where you can be sure of a trouble-free reception.
- **King Abdul Aziz University Hospital** (Old Airport Road).
- **Riyadh Central Hospital** (on Shemaisi Street)—a huge, general hospital that is open to everyone, but most foreigners prefer not to go there.
- **King Fahd National Guard Hospital** (east of Riyadh)— National Guard and families only.
- **Security Forces Hospital** (Siteen Street)—Security Forces and their families only.
- **National Hospital** (Siteen Street)—private.
- **King Khaled Eye Specialist Hospital** (Near Dir'iyah)—the largest eye hospital in the world, but is available to foreigners only by royal order.
- **Dallah Hospital** (excellent private facility).
- **Al Mishari Hospital** (excellent private facility).
- **Al Hamadi Hospital** (private).
- **Mobarak Hospital** (private).
- **Obeid Hospital** (private).
- **Green Crescent** (private).
- **Allied Clinic**—staffed by British and American doctors and dentists and is out-patient only.

Jiddah hospitals

- **Bakhsh Hospital** (Siteen Street).
- **Jiddah Medical Clinic** (behind the Caravan Shopping Centre).

Both of these facilities are recommended, but again, ask your company which you are to use.

Al Khobar hospitals

- **Al Sharq Hospital** (recommended).
- **Al Khobar Central Hospital** (not recommended).
- **Al Salama Hospital** (not recommended).

GENERAL HEALTH FOR FOREIGNERS

Foreigners tend to enjoy relatively good health in this warm, dry land, even though the general level of health and sanitation throughout the country is still lower than in the West. The most common ailments are dysentery, colds and accidents. Serious illness is rare, although we strongly recommend that you have all possible inoculations and vaccinations, regardless of whether or not they are actually required by the authorities. Preventive medicine is always the sensible solution. Smallpox and cholera shots are no longer required, but the cholera shot is still highly recommended. You may also want to consider inoculations for typhus, typhoid, tetanus and polio as well as gamma globulin or new vaccines for hepatitis. Ask your doctor for advice, and also find out how often to have booster shots. Poor sanitation and water supplies, improperly washed foods, and the annual influx of pilgrims from all over the world make adequate vaccinations important.

Malaria is a problem only in the south-western area of the Tihama Plain in the swamps surrounding Jizan. Visitors going to areas of risk are urged to take preventive measures. Ask the company doctor or your clinic about where and when preventive malaria medicine would be necessary. Flies are no longer a problem: an intensive spraying programme has all but eliminated them from the major cities.

It is important not to leave your medical care to chance. Be sure your company has made arrangements for preventive care and for emergency treatment. If you are not employed by a major company, contact your embassy or consulate for information about recommended hospitals, clinics and doctors.

Traditional folk medicine is practised alongside Western medicine in many areas of Saudi Arabia. The practitioners are herb specialists, bleeders and bonesetters. Some of the bonesetters are very good, but the bleeders are nothing less than medieval. Midwifery in remote areas is practised by grandmothers, aunts or the woman down the road. The herbs in the souq are an endless source of fascination. Many strange items are sold for their medicinal value, including ground-up pink scarab beetle for 'tired eyes'. This material is very acidic and after a while burns and scars the cornea of the eye.

Pharmaceuticals

If you have any prescriptions, be sure to take copies written in generic terms, not trade names. Good pharmaceuticals are available (German, US, Japanese, British, and so on), but compounded prescriptions may be difficult to get. Contraceptives are available (German, French, US and English brands).

Many of the imported drugs and medicines that require a prescription in other countries are available over the counter in Saudi Arabia. At any given time, however, a specific item may not be in stock. Items such as sleeping pills or tranquillisers are considered narcotics: you can bring them with you only in very small quantities and only with a doctor's prescription. Basically, if you plan to import any kind of drug, check with the Saudi Consulate for a narcotics permit. This is vitally important.

Dental and eye care

Routine and emergency dental care are both available; however, the better dentists are extraordinarily busy—and expensive. Orthodontics is likely to be a problem. Most Western expatriates have their teeth cared for prior to departure and during home leave.

Dust, the intense light and blowing sand are hard on eyes: treat them with special care. Artificial tears are useful if you have dry eyes. You will definitely need good sunglasses; a large selection is available in Saudi Arabia. Be sure to take prescriptions for glasses and also take an extra pair. It is now possible to have bifocal lenses ground in Saudi Arabia, but it may take some time. In the end it may be just as fast to send your prescription to Europe.

Insurance and health records

When dealing with health insurance claims, keep photocopies of all forms and correspondence. You will be repaid in time, but as at home, correspondence is often prodigious. Keep complete records showing costs, dates, type of service (lab, office, hospital), and a brief description of the complaint. A short letter from your doctor is also helpful.

Expatriates who have lived abroad for long periods recommend that families keep health record books: immunisations, pertinent medical data, drugs taken (when and why), sensitivities or allergies, blood types, and prescriptions for glasses. It is easier to have all the data recorded than to scramble for it if you suddenly need it.

ADJUSTING TO THE HEAT

Most Westerners are not used to the intensity of heat in Saudi Arabia. Not only does it radiate from the sun, but it is also reflected from the earth because there are virtually no trees and little grass to absorb the heat. As if that were not enough, in summertime the winds blow air that is hotter than body temperature—no longer can you assume that a breeze will be cooling.

The heat is uncomfortable, and it can also be harmful—even deadly. Heat exhaustion and heatstroke can quite easily catch the unwary. Since the air is so dry, any moisture quickly evaporates. You will not even notice that you are perspiring but be assured that you are. Sometime, on a very hot day, lick your skin and note how salty it tastes—irrefutable proof of perspiration. Obviously, everyone will need to take in more fluids and more salt than at home. Make it a habit to drink copious amounts of water and soft drinks and to eat salted foods while you live in Saudi Arabia. (Salt tablets are no longer recommended as they can very easily upset the body's electrolyte/fluid balance unless one also drinks large amounts of water.) Lack of salt can lead to faintness, muscle cramps or heatstroke regardless of the temperature. Citrus fruits and bananas provide you with needed potassium. Another good precaution is keeping your head covered when you are in the direct sun. Discuss the matter of heat-related health problems with your doctor before you leave and do some reading on the subject. We give you just a brief description here.

Heat exhaustion

If you see someone suffering from heat exhaustion (with cool and clammy skin and feeling dizzy, nauseous, and weak), put him/her in the shade and elevate the feet to help circulation. If the person can swallow liquids without vomiting, give lightly salted iced water in very small amounts while the person is nauseated. Soak the victim's clothes, and be sure to keep the head wet. This cuts down on further loss of body moisture through perspiration and promotes rapid cooling. Anyone suffering from heat exhaustion will feel ill for several days and must take large amounts of fluid to make up for the losses.

Heatstroke
Heatstroke follows heat exhaustion, but the symptoms are quite different: the skin is dry and hot, not moist and cool, and body temperature is high. Heatstroke is a serious matter and can lead to delirium and death. Put the victim in the shade and do everything possible to reduce the body temperature: loosen the clothing, sponge or sprinkle the person with cool water from head to foot, then vigorously fan the victim and lightly massage arms and legs to restore circulation. If ice is available, pack the victim in it, and above all, get medical help immediately. The principal medical treatment is the lowering of the patient's core temperature as rapidly as possible. This includes spraying with water, fanning, and sometimes involves cool gastric lavage and enemas. Too high a body temperature for any length of time results in irreparable brain damage.

Saudi Arabia is the world leader in the treatment of heatstroke. The Saudis' expertise arises from treating the huge numbers of pilgrims coming into the country each year for the Hajj. When the pilgrimage falls during the summer months, the number of heatstroke victims is mind-boggling. Health officials in Mecca have numerous cooling units located throughout the tent city, and patients are quickly treated and cared for.

Tips for beating the heat
If you arrive in Saudi Arabia during the summer, your body will take from seven to ten days to adapt to the higher temperatures. During this time, take it easy: do not undertake big projects or you will put an added strain on your heart and circulation and make yourself faint, sick, or worse. Even after ten days, avoid over-exertion, particularly if you have a tendency toward high blood pressure. Nowadays, since most houses and cars are air-conditioned, the heat is not such a great problem; still do not underestimate its effect on you. Excessive temperatures last only

from May through September, and in Riyadh the nights cool off except perhaps in July and August.

Cornstarch is good for treating heat rashes. Either mix it with equal parts of water and splash it on your body or add spicy scents (like cinnamon) and powder yourself with it, especially behind the knees or where there are body creases. Cornstarch makes an effective treatment for babies suffering with prickly heat, too.

Running ice cubes over wrists or holding them at the back of your neck will rapidly reduce body heat. Any areas where major arteries are near the surface can be cooled quickly. Some people say that a halved cucumber kept in the refrigerator is very refreshing when run over the face and neck. Another nice touch is to always have ready a bowl of small hand towels or napkins that have been moistened and put into the refrigerator until they are very cold—a great way to welcome people after a hot journey.

When you are at the swimming-pool or out in the sun with exposed areas of skin, be sure to apply a strong sun block every two hours and make sure your children use it too.

FOOD PRECAUTIONS

Vegetables and fruits
With the advent of rapid transportation of fruit and vegetables from the farm to the supermarket, it is seldom necessary to take excessive precautions in their preparation. If you buy from the vegetable markets in the cities, the produce will have been handled several times and should certainly be washed with care. If you are uncertain, soak produce for twenty minutes or so in water with Clorox (about a tablespoon per gallon) or with some other preparation like Milton (a disinfectant, widely available in Saudi Arabia). Then rinse with water that has been sterilised in some manner. Fruit can, of course, simply be rinsed and peeled.

Meat
As in any country, chicken should be cooked with care. Local beef and mutton should also be thoroughly cooked—no rare steaks.

Water
The water supply in the cities has been much improved in the last eight years. Large desalinisation plants on both the east and west coasts process millions of gallons of salt water daily. Water from

the Gulf is piped to Riyadh through three gigantic conduits, six feet in diameter, which run alongside the motorway from Al Khobar to the capital. If you live in the newer sections of any city, the water will be safe to drink. Do not, however, drink the tap water in older sections—it may be brackish or salty. You can buy bottled water or you may choose to purify your tap water with Halizone tablets (or similar preparations) or by boiling it for twenty minutes at an active boil. There are also a number of water filters and purifiers on the market in Europe and the United States which you can attach directly to the tap. Use purified water for ice cubes, toothbrushing and all other oral purposes as well.

Because newly constructed villas are often not connected to the city water system for several months, all are still built with large cisterns to store water for household use. If you live in a new, individual villa, be sure that the water-holding tank, which will be under the front courtyard of your house, is regularly cleaned and disinfected. There may still be seepage and contamination, no matter how well built or new the house is.

9
Leisure

Saudi Arabia offers much that is interesting and enjoyable for people who can provide their own entertainment and who have their own interests. Those who depend almost entirely on outside stimuli (television, sports events, films, concerts, theatres, and so on) will have to work harder to avoid being bored and unhappy. Most of what you do for entertainment in Saudi Arabia you create yourself.

MEDIA ENTERTAINMENT

Films and videos
As the traditionalist movement has grown, so has the disapproval of the showing of films in a setting which encourages large gatherings of foreigners and Saudis together. Videos, however, are popular and are widely available. There are video stores in the cities and large collections in the various international compounds. Some companies maintain extensive video libraries (as well as libraries of English-language books). You can also rent videos from private individuals who have set themselves up in the business. Such rental outlets, however, are illegal—rent from them with care and discretion, that is, do not carry your rented tapes around in public.

Radio, TV, print media
Several radio stations offer programmes, music and religious teachings in Arabic, English, Dutch, German and French. Interestingly, even with the rise of traditionalism, news is censored less than it was previously, and the Kingdom is becoming more open in its broadcasting about current issues. Local news is a bit dull for foreigners as it usually consists of the king's activities for

that day and the weather. If you have a shortwave radio (most foreigners recommend you do), you can pick up the BBC and Voice of America as well as radio stations from Kuwait.

Two national colour TV channels cover the whole country—one in Arabic, the other in English; and ARAMCO has its own channel. In the Eastern Province viewers can pick up the ARAMCO channel as well as a channel from Bahrain, one from Kuwait and one from Qatar. The Saudi English-language channel airs programmes and films along the lines of *I love Lucy*, *Flipper*, and G-rated shows from the United Kingdom and the United States. Films from India are broadcast once a week.

Satellite dishes, permitted in some expatriate compounds, pick up Armed Forces Radio and Television Service (AFRTS), broadcast from Europe. This channel airs only American programmes but does keep one informed about world events and miscellaneous news.

Television has been a powerful educational force in Saudi Arabia: both children's and adult educational programmes are shown daily. That TV is permitted at all is a break with tradition; previously, portrayal of the human form in any manner was forbidden, including the print media.

Newspapers have been on a roller coaster with regard to the publication of women's pictures. Originally, they were forbidden to publish any. Then, after a period of leniency, the boom was lowered again early in 1980, apparently as a concession to the religious leaders. That has changed once again: pictures of women are featured in advertisements in newspapers and magazines, provided, of course, that they are decently clad.

SPORTS

Sports available include tennis, golf, trapshooting, baseball, softball, soccer, basketball and volleyball. Local sports events are held on Fridays (women are not welcome). The traditional sport of the country, especially among wealthy Saudis, is falconry. Imported mostly from Iran and Iraq, falcons are very expensive, a luxury most foreigners cannot afford.

On both coasts, people enjoy sailing, fishing, snorkelling, scuba diving and shelling. Scuba diving and snorkelling in the Red Sea are equal to or better than that offered at the most popular resorts anywhere in the world. Jacques Cousteau is reputed to have said that the Farasan Islands, off the coast from Jizan, have the best diving he has ever seen. In Jiddah the reef is only a few yards from the shore, making it possible for even the most timid to wade out to the edge of the coral and put their faces in the water. The colours of the coral and the huge schools of darting fish are truly awe inspiring. Beware of the sun, though. Snorkelling is so engrossing that it is easy to forget the time. Wear a shirt and long trousers in the water and use sun block. It is far better to feel a bit silly than to suffer from severe sunburn. On trips to the beach take your own sunshade—a big beach umbrella, a tarp, or even a bed sheet with makeshirt poles to support it. As far as snorkelling and diving equipment go, there are several reliable dive shops in Jiddah (and Riyadh) that can supply all your equipment needs for underwater adventures. Diving lessons are also sometimes offered in various compounds. Ask around, read bulletin boards, and take advantage of this great opportunity.

Women at public beaches should wear shirts and long cotton trousers into the water. At private beaches they should wear at least a one-piece suit. In Jiddah the rules are currently very lax, but 'as the wind changes . . .' so may the rules.

Hunting for fossil shells dating from the Jurassic period (180 million years ago) is a favourite activity along the west coast and in the Central District, especially along the Tuwaiq Escarpment. Some fossils are still firmly embedded in the original rock and can be removed only with a hammer and chisel. Less hardy amateur fossil hunters can search along streambeds and at the base of little hillsides to find fossil shells that have broken off from their encasing bed. Along the coast one can find new shells which match those 180 million years old.

ACTIVITIES

There is a large and varied international community in Saudi Arabia and many opportunities to get acquainted and to become as involved as you wish. If you enjoy games, join in evenings of bridge, chess, Ping-Pong, and mah-jong with friends. As we said in an earlier chapter, your stay in Saudi Arabia is the perfect opportunity to enjoy and improve your skills in painting, sewing, cooking, woodworking, and so on. In most cities you will find various kinds of interest groups—stamp collecting, photography, crafts, literary discussion groups, amateur theatre and choral groups, to name just a few. Many people keep productively busy for many hours a week doing research or pursuing special studies. The archaeology—or history of geology—of Saudi Arabia is a popular area of interest, as is the study of Islam. There is the story of a Canadian woman who spent two years in Riyadh reading steadily and purposefully through a multivolumed encyclopaedia that she had taken with her. Other wives used to join her regularly for quiet reading parties. Many large US state universities offer correspondence courses, some with degree credit. Classes are available in Arabic as well as other languages. Some expatriates bring self-instructional tapes, records and books. Others offer informal classes in their areas of interest and skill. In Riyadh, contact the American Community Services office (463 4007) for information about continuing education, workshops and counselling.

Saudi Arabia is not a particularly exciting place for single men—there are few single Western women. Married couples and families fare better. Riyadh and most of the other inland cities in Saudi Arabia are much more restrained and strict than Jiddah or Dhahran; their people are less accustomed to foreigners than the citizens of both coasts.

Clubs and organisations

Jiddah has a Natural History Society, a choral society, and two amateur theatrical groups for adults, as well as one for children. There is also a light opera company, a barbershop quartet, a computer club, and clubs for swimming, bowling, riding and diving.

Riyadh also offers the International Arts and Crafts Society, the Nautical Society, the Natural History Society, a theatrical group (The Riyadh Players), a sports club and a concert band.

In the Dhahran area of the Eastern Province are the ARAMCO Aquarium Society, an art group, a choral society, a camera club, a diving club, a garden club, a folk dance group, a horse association, a computer club, a theatre group and a golf club. Sports enthusiasts will find a number of organised sports, such as aerobics, judo, karate, running, rugby, soccer, softball, tennis and Little League.

We should mention that theatrical groups are frowned upon by the religious authorities and therefore keep a low profile. Square dancing is also by necessity a clandestine activity, but the three major cities (Riyadh, Jiddah and Al Khobar) have very active square dance groups. Take your shoes, however, since they are not available in the Kingdom.

These lists of organisations are by no means exhaustive since new ones are constantly being formed. We recommend that soon after your arrival, you obtain a copy of one of the following excellent booklets from your embassy, your company's personnel office, or a women's club: 'Welcome to Jiddah', 'Welcome to Riyadh', 'Welcome to Dhahran', and 'A Practical Guide to the Eastern Province of Saudi Arabia'.

In addition to recreation and organisations, these booklets cover such topics as dress, laws, etiquette, schools, health, transportation, weather, shopping and travel.

Desert outings

If you like the desert, Saudi Arabia offers endless opportunities for exploration or just casual outings. The best time of the year for visiting the desert is between October and April when the temperatures are more comfortable than during the summer months. Indeed, January can be downright cold for camping out. But you must take the desert seriously. It can fascinate you, but it can just as easily kill you. Take more fluids to drink than you think you could possibly need. Also, pack a tow rope, compass, shovel, small mirror to use as a flash signal if you are in trouble, and a lightweight sheet or tarp to use for shade should the necessity arise. Always go with other people and take two cars. Once in the desert, do not walk out of sight of the car or the road. If you choose to go into the deep desert, ask some seasoned 'desert rats' to go with you and follow their lead. Always tell someone where you are going and when you expect to be back. Then keep to your plans and report in when you get home.

Be sure to wear hats and use a sun block. Watch children closely in the desert. They can rapidly become dehydrated and, without complaining or crying, may quietly go to sleep, fade away, and die. However, if they have plenty of water and are properly clad, they will be fine.

If your car breaks down (and you have not travelled with another vehicle) or if for any other reason you find yourself marooned on the desert, follow these basics of desert survival:

● DO NOT PANIC. Panicking uses up a great deal of energy,

which in turn wastes water, not to mention the effect it has on decision-making.

- STAY WITH THE CAR. If your car breaks down, stay with it. Here are some reasons why:

  1. Cars are easily visible from afar, both on the ground and from the air; humans alone are practically invisible.
  2. The car contains all you need to survive, and you cannot possibly carry these necessities for any distance, especially in the heat of the day.
  3. Most people cannot walk more than twenty kilometres in one day, and then only in ideal conditions, so you will not get very far should you decide to walk out of the desert.
  4. Away from the car you have no protection from the sun or from thorns and insects.
  5. It is impossible to carry all the water you need for fluid replacement as you trudge along.

     The exception to this rule is if you can see help close by. Don't be fooled, however, by areas of new farms. Many of them may look inhabited but may in fact be abandoned. They might, however, be a source of water. If you do decide, against all odds, to walk for help, leave a note on the steering wheel of your car telling your rescuers when you left and in which direction (the sighting from your compass) you went; then stick to that sighting. Rescuers will then know if they should rush to your rescue or have tea before searching for your bodies.

- SIGNAL FOR HELP. Light a fire at night; during the day a burning tyre (deflated) makes an excellent smoke signal. To get the fire going, douse the tyre with petrol, but **be careful**.
- FIND OR MAKE SHADE. Using your vehicle as the back wall, you can rig a makeshift lean-to with your tarp or sheet and two sturdy poles (which you should bring along).
- DRINK FLUIDS but not wastefully. Drink small amounts at regular intervals. Do not eat. The body requires fluids for the metabolism of food and if water is in short supply, it is better to forgo eating for a day or two.
- KEEP YOUR SPIRITS UP. The desert in Saudi Arabia is surprisingly full of people and, even though the situation looks hopeless, all you need do is attract their attention and they will come to your rescue.

Other outdoor activities
The Tuwaiq Escarpment in the Central District is a wonderful
place for camping and hiking in the endless network of box
canyons. (Camping gear is available but it is cheaper to bring your
own from home.) The limestone and sandstone cliffs provide
challenges for rock climbers. If you are an outdoor person, you
may want to consider buying a four-wheel-drive vehicle for your
personal use. Not only does it give you access to faraway places,
it provides an added element of protection in the event of accidents.

Once the hub of world trade routes, Saudi Arabia is rich in
antiquities: rock drawings and ancient abandoned villages and cities
to explore. You may come upon Stone Age settlements dating back
eight to ten thousand years. With permission from the Ministry of
Antiquities you may visit Al Fau, a Nabatean city, which was a
commercial centre on the great caravan routes of Arabia Felix
2,000 years ago. You can also visit the site of Rabadah on the
Darb Zubaidah, a more recent city, which was destroyed by the
Carpathians in AD 800 (200 AH by the Islamic calendar). These
and other archaeological sites that have lain undisturbed for one
to two thousand years are now being carefully excavated by teams
of scientists from the University of Riyadh.

Bird watching
The Arabian Peninsula supports an amazingly prolific bird population. Many birds are permanent residents, especially since the
advent of extensive farming in the Central Province, and many
other species fly over the peninsula on their annual migration
routes. The best sites for bird-watching are around Riyadh at the
manmade lakes of Mansouriyah on the Riyadh River or in the
vicinity of any of the large pivot fields in the escarpment valley
and around Al Kharj. Binoculars are available and are about the
same price as at home.

The Desert Ramblers in Riyadh has taken a new name, the
Riyadh Natural History Society. It sponsors lectures about the
birdlife and wildlife of Arabia, and on occasion the members
organise desert outings.

ACTIVITIES FOR WOMEN

A woman recently returned from living in Saudi Arabia gave this
advice for expatriate wives:

When you get there, join one or more of the clubs, attend several meetings, and sit rather quietly but listen hard. Keep your mouth closed but your eyes and ears open for the first several weeks. It is best not to jump into anything too fast but to wait until you are ready, then volunteer your services in whatever appeals to you most and do it well. Everything else will follow.

My biggest advice to anyone, however, is to avoid gossip. Let all the rumours you hear drop at your feet; don't pass them on. In a closed community rumours fly, and it does no one any good. If all women would really take this to heart, they could stop 99 percent of the rumours from circulating at all.

As to the Saudi women, never underestimate their power; they are bright. Don't push or preach or look down on them. Accept their ancient and lovely culture as it is. If they want to change any parts of it, they will—in their own way. They do not need outsiders telling them anything. Westerners tend to be terribly condescending just because the Saudi women wear veils. That is a real mistake.

In short, my advice is be quiet, relax, enjoy, get into the flow. It is very different, but it is a wonderful culture, a wonderful people, and a great experience to be there.

Clubs

In Jiddah there are two active women's clubs for the expatriate community: the **American Ladies of Jiddah**, for women who are US citizens or married to US citizens, and the **International Women's Club**, for women of nationalities other than American. Both clubs offer lectures, luncheons and activity/interest groups, such as bridge, cooking, exercise/yoga and trips to places of interest.

Two Saudi women's organisations in Jiddah are open to foreign women:

1. **Jame'lya Ta'awuniyya** (Women's Co-operative Centre) offers classes in both Arabic and English and also teaches dressmaking. There are monthly cultural programmes for Saudi women and members of the international community. The centre sponsors a nursery school for about eighty children of low-income families, run by members.
2. **Jaami'at Al-Nissa' Al-Hurriyah** (Free Institute of Women)

is a welfare group offering classes in English, Arabic, sewing, and so on. It sponsors a beauticians' school, operates a day-care centre, and has a food distribution programme.

There used to be an International Women's Club in Riyadh, but at the direction of the religious police (due to some 'objectionable' comments made by one of the speakers), it was disbanded. At the time of writing there are no publicised women's clubs in Riyadh, but things change from moment to moment, and one may have already sprung up by the time we go to print. Ask around after you arrive: you never know what will turn up.

Sewing
Many women enjoy sewing, embroidering, and doing other stitchery together in small groups in one another's homes. You can purchase embroidery thread and yarns, but you may want to take a good supply of your own anyway. Take your own knitting needles, crochet hooks, patterns, zippers, buttons, thread, and canvas and patterns for needlepoint.

Gardening
Jiddah is a particularly good place to garden. If plants grow there at all, they grow with enthusiasm and in all seasons. Good gardeners take the time and trouble to learn what plants like the Saudi climate. Since gardens need watering daily, gardeners tend to spend quite a bit of time tending their plants.

October is the normal planting time, but seeds can be started any time (available from local nurseries). A great many seed-eating birds migrate over the Red Sea area, and many an unprotected garden has been lost to them.

Volunteering
Expatriate wives can find plenty of opportunities to volunteer their time in the international community. They can work in clinics or schools; hold orientation sessions for newly arrived expatriate families; and/or organise activities such as art shows, glee clubs, children's parties, and the like within the international community. Those who have the requisite skill can give lessons in their home in piano, bridge, dressmaking, languages, typing, and so on.

One wife developed a full life for herself by speaking English with Saudi wives in their homes and reading to their children to help them practise their English, thus getting to know a number of Saudi families very well.

Foreign women and jobs

Formerly, expatriate wives could work in foreign firms in Saudi Arabia. With only a few exceptions, this is no longer true. Since the influence of the religious leaders has grown, the government has written to many major foreign companies, warning them against employing women in any capacity other than nursing or teaching. The penalty is a jail term for the employer and immediate expulsion of the woman and her husband. Women wanting work should try to make arrangements in advance and enter the country with a visa from a sponsoring company.

ACTIVITIES FOR CHILDREN

The lives of young expatriate children in Saudi Arabia are somewhat different from what they are accustomed to at home, though most quickly adapt to the new situation. Children who live in apartment houses in cities have to adjust to a life that is fairly curtailed: traffic is dangerous, and they cannot venture out alone. In Western compounds, however, they can run quite freely. Many living quarters are walled in, providing a protected play area; mothers know where their children are and with whom they are playing. Mothers often take turns watching each other's children as well as taking groups of children to swim, ride or participate in other activities. Most compounds are designed to include play-grounds. Many new parks have been built which have the same kind of equipment that children are accustomed to at home: swings, slides, and jungle gyms. However, parks are sandy and grass is a luxury.

School-age children's lives centre primarily on their school, school friends, sports and other activities geared toward their age group. Swimming-pools are everywhere: every child who is in-terested should be able to return home from Saudi Arabia as a swimming and diving expert. If children are interested in scouting, they will find plenty of Cub Scout, Brownie, Boy Scout and Girl Scout troops. Little League players will need a good supply of baseball gloves and balls.

Most families go to another country to escape the heat during summer holidays. Teenagers are apt to travel, get jobs outside Saudi Arabia, take part in one of Europe's many workcamps, or take summer courses in Switzerland, England or elsewhere.

10
Cities in Profile

RIYADH

Riyadh (which is Arabic for 'gardens') is the country's political capital and the seat of government: see Map 2. Once a sleepy desert town situated on the east side of the beautiful, well-watered Wadi Hanifah, it was surrounded by small villages, and the area was lush with date groves, grainfields, and apricot and pomegranate orchards. The royal city has now become a metropolis of government ministries, high-rise buildings, palaces, schools and hospitals, and is the largest city in the country. Suburbs, complete with shopping malls, sprawl out across the plains and provide homes for the nearly two million people of the city. Approximately 293 square miles in area, Riyadh spreads east across the adjacent plateau towards the Buwayb Escarpment, west far beyond the edge of the Wadi Hanifah and north to Dir'iyah.

The contrast between modern twentieth-century culture and the traditional, isolated culture of Islamic Saudi Arabia is as marked in Riyadh as anywhere in the world. Massive building projects, thousands of American and Japanese cars, and shops flowing with Western luxuries balance precariously against strictly puritanical tradition. An example of this paradox is the large square beside the Friday Mosque and in front of the Palace of Justice (the courthouse), which on most days serves as a car-park but on rare occasions is the city's execution ground.

The international airport, about 30 kilometres north of the city, is beautiful, airy and well designed. It is a pleasure to arrive at this lovely airport, which has two international and two domestic terminals. The terminals lead the flow of travellers down escalators, past gardens and fountains, through the rather tedious immigration lines, to baggage claim, and out via customs.

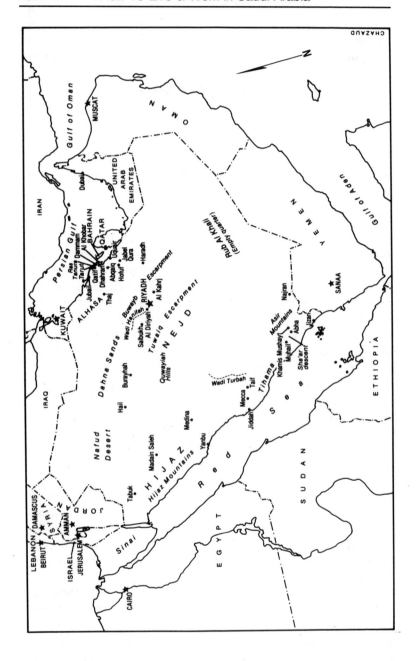

The next surprise is Airport Road, the six-lane motorway leading into the city. Circled by a ring road, Riyadh is also crossed from north to south by Highway 65 and from east to west by Highway 40. Well maintained and brightly lit, these motorways are part of the infrastructure of newly completed highways crisscrossing the Kingdom. Flying in at night, one sees city lights stretching from horizon to horizon, glowing orange in the faint but ever present dust pall hanging over Riyadh.

King Abdul Aziz Road (also known as Old Airport Road) still houses many of the ministries (government departments), but as the city has grown the ministries have moved into new quarters. These are scattered about in the vicinity of Nassiriyah to be near the main government cabinet complex.

South-east of the city is the futuristic sports stadium, looking rather like a spaceship, where the Saudis hope one day to host the Olympic games. To the south is the industrial area with a large cement plant, various light industries and the animal souqs.

In the north-eastern quarter of the city is Nassiriyah, the most beautiful and affluent residential part of Riyadh. Here one will find most of the royal palaces, some of them quite dazzling. In this district the new government cabinet complex has been built. It lies west of the Dir'iyah Road (to Salbukh and points north) and south of Highway 40 (to Mecca, Taif, and points west of Riyadh). The buildings are designed in modernistic concrete Nejd style (solid walls with crenellated tops). The main conference palace and the Friday Mosque are in modified medieval Islamic style, which is quite magnificent, with the buildings finished in copper and ceramic tiles. Gleaming in the desert sun, the colours and symmetry of these beautiful buildings are quite breathtaking.

Adjacent to the cabinet complex but on the north side of Highway 40 is the new Diplomatic Quarter, a spacious maze of streets, parks, gardens, pools (including a wave pool), and sports facilities. The 1,600 acres (650 hectares) is home to some eighty embassies and consulates plus housing for their staff members. There is also a commerical centre with shops, banks, and restaurants. The delightful desert landscaping, featuring native and imported plants, is watered by recycled 'excess' water stored in one of the two large water towers which dominate the quarter's horizon.

Also in the north-east of Riyadh, east of the motorway is King Saud University. Another architectural masterpiece, this lovely

Table 10.1 Average Celsius Temperatures of selected Middle Eastern Cities

City	Jan	Feb	Mar	Apr	May	Jun	July	Aug	Sep	Oct	Nov	Dec
Manama, Bahrain	16	16	20	24	29	31	33	34	31	28	26	25
Beirut	13	14	15	18	21	24	26	27	26	23	19	15
Cairo	13	14	17	20	25	27	29	28	26	24	20	15
Dhahran	17	17	21	25	30	33	35	35	32	28	32	18
Dubai	18	19	21	24	28	31	33	33	31	27	24	20
Jiddah	24	24	24	27	29	30	32	32	31	29	27	25
Kuwait City	14	15	19	25	30	35	36	37	33	27	20	15
Medina	18	20	24	27	34	34	36	42	34	30	23	20
Riyadh	15	15	21	25	30	33	35	35	32	27	20	16
Taif	15	15	19	21	21	29	32	27	27	22	18	16

university with many faculties is for men only. Women are educated on the old campus in downtown Riyadh.

Many years ago city planners decided that Riyadh should grow out but not up. Consequently, the few clusters of tall buildings in the commercial areas stand out as great landmarks which, along with Panda stores and Dunkin' Donuts, will help you find your way around. Street names and house numbers are being put in at this time but all will be in Arabic and will not be much help to expatriate residents.

Climate
Riyadh's climate is dry, healthy and pleasant. August and September are the hottest months but are not unbearably so. See Table 10.1. Winter weather can be quite cold and spring storms may bring torrential downpours which will fill up all the little waterways, creating unexpected waterfalls and sometimes flash floods. Many of the streets were not designed with adequate drainage, and during these storms lower areas fill with water, becoming impassable. If you get stuck in such a place, wade to the side of the road and wait until the pumper trucks come along to clean up the mess. This may, of course, be several hours, but it is inadvisable to leave your car unguarded as it will be towed away when it is reachable.

Shopping
The main commercial area was, at one time, King Faisal Road (also known as Wazir Street) in the old downtown. Now there are several large shopping centres scattered throughout the city. One, in Ulayah, is the fountain-bedecked Al Akhariyah Mall which has an enormous collection of shops selling everything from shoes to music tapes, jewellery to linens, and clothing. There are two fairly small department stores, a Wrangler Jeans shop, and a Benetton knitwear outlet. Prices vary, of course, but are comparable to London or New York. East of the city is the used-car souq, where many small dealers sell everything from Suzukis to Lamborghinis. Near Justice Square and in Batha are the old souqs and numerous reliable money-changers.

Places of interest
In the old downtown area of Riyadh, several buildings are of interest: the Murabba Palace of Abdul Aziz (partially restored),

the Muzmak Fort in the Dira souq, and the lovely Red Palace (restored and still used as working offices). For those interested in the history of the peninsula, there is a small but excellent museum on Imam Saud ibn Abdul Aziz ibn Muhammad Street (yes, that is a real street name), also known as the Old Mecca Road. The museum leads one from prehistoric times to the Islamic era. The bookshop carries copies of *Atlal*, the Department of Antiquities research journal. Of the many new buildings, the television tower is of special interest, and tours of the facility, especially for schoolchildren, may be arranged.

Dining out
Riyadh boasts many excellent hotels, including the Marriott, the Intercontinental, the Riyadh Palace and the Al Khozama. All of the major hotels in Saudi Arabia serve scrumptious Friday brunches. Catering mostly to the expatriate population, the food is cosmopolitan and delicious. Throughout the city are many ethnic restaurants from countries around the world. Health Department regulations are strict and all eating establishments are inspected regularly.

Excursions
The scenery surrounding Riyadh is impressive, with red sand dunes, buttes and spires in the Dirab Valley which are somewhat similar to Monument Valley in Arizona.

About fifty kilometres south of the capital is the green and lovely farming community of Al Kharj. The abundant waters of the area are pumped from the immense underground aquifer which extends from Najran to Al Kharj and then flows east through Haradh to the Gulf. A ruined palace in Al Kharj provides a fine example of Nejd mud construction.

On the north-west corner of Riyadh, and on the edge of Wadi Hanifah, lies the ancient capital of Al Dir'iyah. Destroyed by the Egyptians in 1818, Al Dir'iyah is a fascinating archaeological site, which has been extensively excavated and partially restored by the Department of Antiquities from the University of Riyadh.

Further south is the Wadi Hanifah, a perennial stream that carries the well-treated effluent from the city. After flowing through wetlands now protected and designated as a bird refuge, the river eventually soaks into the Ak Kharj Aquifer.

Leisure Activities

In addition to the activities and organizations mentioned in chapter 9, the following are specific to Riyadh:

- **Drama** The Riyadh Players Little Theatre Group (for expatriates only) puts on five or six major performances a year.
- **Spectator Sports**. During the cooler months the Malaz Stadium has weekly camel and horse races. Soccer games, often featuring international teams, are played every Friday. Women are welcome at the races but not at soccer games.
- **Sports clubs and gymnasiums**. These are similar to athletic clubs anywhere, but some allow female members, with separate days for men and women. There are several places to go bowling, the Intercontinental Hotel being one.

JIDDAH (or Jidda or Jeddah)

Jiddah means 'bride of the sea', a fitting name for the key port on the Red Sea, and is the largest city in the Kingdom. It lies on a flat, sandy stretch of coast about halfway between Suez and Aden. A prebiblical city with no natural vegetation, it is now a cosmopolitan metropolis of glass and steel buildings with a superb manmade corniche (beachfront road, park and walkway) around the waterfront. Until thirty years ago Jiddah could not expand because of a limited supply of drinking water. Then a water system was installed and later a desalinisation plant, so that finally Jiddah had as much water as it needed. In 1950 the great city walls were pulled down, and Jiddah began its incredible spiral of growth. It has become so cosmopolitan—partly because of the port and partly because for many years it was the diplomatic centre—that its culture is closest of all Saudi cities to that of the West. As a result, the influx of Westerners has caused less shock than in Riyadh and other cities.

At the last count the population was estimated at 2.5 million. The city was vastly overbuilt in the early 1980s, and as a result many villas and compounds are empty and rents are quite cheap.

In Jiddah the new King Khaled International Airport (KKIA), located 35 kilometres north of town, was opened in December 1983. Though not as beautiful as the airport in Riyadh, it is quite efficient and comfortable. It has three main terminals: domestic, international, and the beautiful Hajj terminal located at the north end of the runways. This terminal, used only once a year by the million or so pilgrims to Mecca, is a huge structure consisting of a series of tent-shaped roofs supported by pillars. The whole building is without walls or seats and is cooled by giant ceiling fans. There is also a royal terminal for the ruling family and visiting dignitaries.

At one time the Jiddah airport claimed to be the largest in the world, but it has since been outstripped by Riyadh and will soon rank third when the new airport in Dhahran is completed. Do not take any pictures of this or any other airport building in Saudi Arabia.

An outstanding motorway system serves Jiddah. The Ring Road circles the city, with huge highways leading to Mecca and Medina.

Once a world of ornate wood balconies, casements, lattices and screens overhanging narrow, winding streets, the lovely old style of Jiddah is fast disappearing. Although a few buildings have been preserved, the majority have given way to tall, gleaming sky-scrapers which now dominate the bustling city. Around the downtown area are suburbs where most of the residents live, including the large international community.

Life is quite pleasant in Jiddah. There are well-stocked shops and a great variety of restaurants. Behind compound walls social life thrives. Despite the cultural limitations, there is plenty to do here. On any weekend one can enjoy the mountains, beaches or desert. The Red Sea is superb for snorkelling and scuba diving. The Al Bilad Hotel on the corniche has two private beaches, and just off Obhur Creek, north of town, are beautiful reefs. Several sailing clubs are based in the creek itself, and although several hotels were planned for the creek, as yet none of them has been built.

As Jiddah grew, city planners went ahead and built blocks of streets, put in services, then waited for the land to be sold and built up. A huge sculpture was built at each of the major intersections in these embryo suburbs. They are useful when giving instructions to a limousine or taxi driver.

The corniche along the Red Sea extends for 8 miles to the north. Local sculptors were given free rein, and at intervals all along the sea wall are works of art which vary from ugly to unique to awe-inspiring. There are several amusement parks—for families only—and several large hotels that cater for the beach crowd. Many of these hotels have snorkelling and scuba equipment for rent, but one must be a certified diver to rent scuba gear. In 1988 construction began on the south corniche which is past the Royal Saudi Naval Base.

There used to be a lagoon in the heart of the city, but that has now mostly been filled in. The small remaining body of water displays the beautiful, 300-foot-high Jiddah fountain. The fishing dhows and boat-building yards have been moved to make way for the corniche.

A good way to see the city when you are new is to take the city bus. Part of the SAPTCO system, these red and blue buses cost two riyals a ride, run every few minutes, make frequent stops and travel in a large circle, eventually ending up where you started.

Climate
Jiddah is warm and humid (often rising over 90 per cent). The temperature climbs to over 100 degrees in the summer months; thankfully, air-conditioning is standard in residences, and all compounds have swimming pools.

Shopping
Of the many malls in Jiddah, the best is the International Market. Here one can find bookstores, camera and stereo equipment, clothing, and many places to eat. Another good mall is the Middle East Market next to the Marriott Hotel. The newest at the time of writing, the Jampoon Centre, is next to the Red Sea and two blocks from the US Consulate. Housed in a huge building, the mall is very beautiful and worth visiting just to enjoy the architecture, even if you do not want to buy anything. As in Riyadh, there are still the old intriguing souqs, where you can buy gold, carpets, antiques and water-pipes (hubble-bubbles). Beware of the last item as these may be confiscated by US Customs as drug paraphernalia.

Food markets
Major supermarkets include Tamimi and Fouad, Sarawat and Caravan. Also, there are numerous fresh produce markets, fish markets and butcher shops. In several malls and shopping complexes one can find pastry shops and fast-food outlets.

Dining out
Jiddah is packed with places to eat. All the major hotels have excellent restaurants, especially the Red Sea Palace (downtown), the Al Bilad (on the corniche), and the Marriott (Palestine Road).

They all have sumptuous Friday brunches. Close to the Jamjoon Centre is the Twin Dolphin Restaurant, which has a wonderful view of the great coloured fountain in the lagoon. One can also choose among the many ethnic restaurants, which offer good food.

Excursions

If you like the outdoors, the west coast will delight you. A long weekend trip to Al Sawdah National Park in the vicinity of Abha is a total surprise, with breathtaking mountain scenery, quiet forests and wild animals. Taif, on top of the escarpment, is the summer capital and a lovely spot for a weekend getaway. Madain Salih and the Hijaz Railway can both be taken in on one trip to the north. For this you need a travel permit obtainable from the Directorate-General of Antiquities and Museums, PO Box 3734, Riyadh 11481. You can go with a package tour or on your own, but if you go solo, be sure to take everything you need, including water (see 'Desert outings', chapter 9).

All along the coast are lovely picnic spots and places to go snorkelling, but before you strike out on your own, check first with other expatriates to find out where and when to go.

Leisure activities

For men and women alike, the sky is the limit on water sports. There is the Red Sea sailing Club, deep-sea fishing, wind surfing, diving and snorkelling. Several excellent dive shops in Jiddah can supply all your equipment needs, arrange for boats if you want to go further out to dive in unspoiled areas, and provide instruction for beginners. Red Sea Divers, the largest and best dive store, has three shops in town, the biggest located behind the main Safeway. Diving and snorkelling in the Red Sea are unparallelled anywhere in the world, an opportunity not to be passed up.

Various social clubs are attached to consulates and companies, and outsiders may attend when accompanied by a member. Some hotels open their pools on a fee basis to non-guests, but a government decree bars women from using public pools.

YANBU

Located 350 miles north of Jiddah, Yanbu is one of the two new manufacturing cities built by the government. An industrial complex has been built at Yanbu to shift the oil industry away from the strategically vulnerable Gulf. Construction began in 1977 and is now mostly complete. Oil and gas to be processed here comes across country from the east coast via huge pipelines. Foreign technologists and young Saudi engineers work with state- of-the-art equipment and live in neighbourhoods that look like scenes transported from the Arizona desert.

EASTERN PROVINCE: Dhahran, Al Khobar and Dammam

Dhahran

Dhahran, on the east coast, is about 280 miles from Riyadh and 1,000 miles from Jiddah. The name *Dhahran* referred originally only to the ARAMCO community that was established about forty years ago after ARAMCO's first discovery of oil. The Dhahran airport is smaller than those of Riyadh or Jiddah, but it is still spacious. Its design is striking, appearing like a series of white canvas tents or waves. It is frequently mentioned as a superb example of modern architecture.

Dhahran is a replica of a US suburb with rows of neat modern houses, schools, recreation facilities, a library, family and bachelor housing, a hospital and a dental clinic. There are snack bars, pools, tennis courts, an eighteen-hole, oil-sand golf course, specially designed jogging and exercising trails, a commissary, a post office, lush green lawns, a hobby farm (for riding and so on), and a twelve-lane bowling alley—all for use by ARAMCO employees and their guests. A spacious yacht club and swimming and beach facilities are located at Half Moon Bay, 21 kilometres south of town.

The US Consulate, just outside Dhahran, is also the location of Dhahran Academy. Dhahran International Airport and the King Abdul Aziz Military Airport, both near the city, border each other and use the same runways. As soon as the new King Fahd International Airport is completed in 1992, these two airports will revert strictly to military installations. Close by the airports is the fabulous Dhahran International Hotel.

Bordering Dhahran on the east is the King Fahd Petroleum and Minerals University, formerly known as UPM (University of Petroleum and Minerals).

Al Khobar

About 7 miles south-east of Dhahran is the city of Al Khobar, stretching along the shore of the Gulf. A separate and distinct community, Al Khobar is a cosmopolitan shopping and business centre with major hotels, restaurants and markets. It is a city of air-conditioned apartments with a veritable jungle of TV antennae on the rooftops. The corniche is undergoing a major beautification programme to provide gardens and recreational facilities along the entire length of Al Khobar's beachfront. South of the city is the private Sunset Yacht Club, and adjacent to the Meridian Hotel, a public yacht club is being built. The original small harbour strewn with fishing boats is hardly recognisable today. With the opening of the Saudi-Bahraini Causeway, the peaceful harbour and many of the beautiful old dhows which ferried people back and forth across the water have now vanished. And most of the fishing boat docks have given way to a large customs facility.

The population of this ultramodern city is made up of Arabs, Asians, Europeans and Americans, most of whom are involved with local trading and related businesses, service companies on contract to Saudi ARAMCO, or major construction projects—for example, Bechtel and the new King Fahd Airport.

Dammam

Eleven miles north of Al Khobar and still on the Gulf is the capital of Al Hasa (the Eastern Province), Dammam. This city, with its enormous modern port, has numerous restaurants, shops, industrial parks and government buildings. The Saudi Railroad starts here and travels to Riyadh with stops in Dhahran, Abqaiq, Hofuf, Haradh and Al Kharj. The passenger trains are quiet and very fast. This same railroad also services the port, which stretches 11 miles into the Gulf. Here ships can unload cargo directly onto freight cars or trucks. Off-loading time for major cargo vessels is less than twenty-four hours, substantially less time than at conventional port facilities. The port also has huge storage facilities, maintenance shops and floating dry docks.

His Royal Highness, Prince Muhammad ibn Fahd, Governor of the Eastern Province, holds court in Dammam but lives in Al Khobar. Prior to the oil boom, both these cities were small scruffy fishing villages, but today are clean, modern towns where garbage is collected twice daily. As in any modern city, traffic is congested at rush hours. Drainage is good, but during the rare thunderstorm flooding may occur, and it is advisable to avoid flooded areas until the water has receded.

Climate
Temperatures are hotter than in the interior, and the humidity in July, August and September is stifling. The shammal (north wind), which blows almost continually in June and July, produces major dust and sandstorms.

Shopping
Dammam has a large shopping mall with numerous shops selling a wide variety of international goods. Furniture of all kinds is available at reasonable prices. Small and large appliances, stereos, TVs, VCRs and cameras are all cheap and plentiful. Safeway-style supermarkets are the norm, and fresh fish and vegetable souqs ply a very busy trade.

Television and radio
The Eastern Province offers more TV and radio channels than anywhere else in the country: the Saudi Arabic and English channels, the ARAMCO channel, Bahrain, Qatar and Kuwait. Four FM stations broadcast from ARAMCO and at least one from Kuwait, which plays American top-forty hits.

Excursions
If you love the outdoors and camping, the east coast, like the rest of Saudi Arabia, has much to offer. Hofuf, in the centre of Al Hasa, is one of the world's largest oases and is only about two hours away by car. Its lovely shady farms, running water and prolific bird life are a refreshing change from the city. In the town is a great Thursday market, where you can find all kinds of antiques, handicrafts and brassware. Deep in the oasis is the rather strange mountain (it is really only a little hill), Jabel Qara, with miles of cool, sinister caves. On one side of Jabel Qara is a village of pottery-makers. Their work is sun-dried, not kiln-fired. People have lived here for thousands of years, and there are many archaeological sites. At one time this area was a very important stopping-place along the trade routes from the coast. This area is inhabited by a great many Shi'ite Muslims, the sect predominant in the news over the past few years, and disturbances have occurred on several occasions. The region is considered somewhat unstable.

About an hour and a half south along the coast, Uqair's decaying port facilities and a huge Turkish fort offer another interesting excursion. From here the camel caravans went straight over the sand dunes to the great oasis of Hofuf. The road is made of friable rock from the beaches of the Gulf and is still clearly visible today as it wanders over the dune crests. With a great deal of skill, a super four-wheel-drive vehicle and a good compass, one can follow this track to Al Hasa. The most interesting aspect of the road is that it is littered with potsherds. Who knows what other treasures may lie along this ancient and much-travelled road?

North of Al Khobar is Qatif with the interesting island of Tarut just offshore. This island, connected to the mainland by a short causeway and harbouring evidence of Neolithic inhabitants, is thought to be the oldest settlement on the peninsula. Further north is Thaj, an archaeological site dating from the seventh century BC, which was already a ruin by the time of the advent of Islam. Like Hofuf, Qatif has a great outdoor market, where one can buy fresh fish, produce, and local handicrafts.

With the completion of the Saudi-Bahraini Causeway, a trip to Bahrain is as simple as getting an exit/re-entry visa and driving across the bay. Here you can buy a cocktail, see a film or go dancing. Women can rent a car and drive all over the island. In Bahrain there are also many archaeological sites of great interest.

Leisure activities throughout the Eastern Province
Trips by dhow may be made to various islands in the Gulf, and if you join a yacht club and buy your own boat, you can spend many happy leisure hours on the Gulf waters. Modern beach facilities are available all the way from south of Al Khobar (Half Moon Bay) to Dammam, with expansion planned as far north as Tarut Island. When finished, the corniche will be 80 kilometres in length. The public beaches south of Al Khobar offer fishing, waterskiing and sailing, as well as swimming. Some of the hotels have swimming-pool clubs. There are large state-of-the-art sports facilities open to the general public. Women may use them on specific days.

JUBAIL

The Gulf city of Jubail is located sixty kilometres north of Ras Tanura and was the first industrial petrochemical city in Saudi Arabia. It has modern exporting facilities at both the New

Industrial Port and the New Commercial Port. Modern housing
and city services are available for all nationalities. There is a regular
charter bus service available between Jubail and Al Khobar.

Glossary

'Afwan. You're welcome/not at all.

Ahlan wa sahlan! Welcome!

Alhamdulillah. Thanks be to God.

Amir. Governor of a province.

Baksheesh. Gratuity.

Bismillah. In the name of God.

Eid al Adha. Feast of the Sacrifice.

Eid al Fitr. Feast of the Breaking of the Fast.

Fi aman allah. (Go) in the care of God.

Hajj. Pilgrimage to Mecca.

Hegira. Emigration.

Ibn. Son (of).

Igama. Residency permit.

Ijma. Consensus as a source of Islamic law.

Imam. Prayer/congregation leader.

Inshallah. If God wills.

Islam. Submission to God.

Ma'a salaama. Goodbye.

Majlis. Open court.

Malik. King.

Marhaba. Hello.

Marhabtayn. Two hellos (reply).

Masa' al-khayr. Good evening.

Masa' an-nuur. Evening of light (reply).

Muezzin. One who calls the Muslims to prayer.

Mutawwa'een. Religious police.

Qadi. Judge.

Qiyas. Logical deduction from the Holy **Qur'an** and **sunna**.

Qur'an. 'The Reading', i.e. the Holy Book of **Islam**.

Ramadan. Month of fasting.

Sabaah al-khayr. Good morning.

Sabaah an-nuur. Morning of light (reply).

Shammal. Strong north-west wind in spring and autumn.

Shari'a. Islamic law.

Sheikh. Tribal leader.

Shesha. Water-pipe (hookah).

Shukran. Thanks.

Shukran jazilan. Thank you very much.

Sidiqui. Homemade raw alcohol.

Souq. Bazaar.

Sunna. Practices of the Prophet Muhammad.

Ulema. Religious scholars.

Wadi. Huge dry river-bed.

Zakat. Tax of 2.5 per cent of a Muslim's income, to be distributed among the poor.

Further Reading

CULTURAL/EDUCATIONAL

'Antar and 'Abla, a Bedouin Romance, Diane Richmond (ed.) (Quartet Books, 1978). A delightful collection of tales from the pre-Islamic era, telling of love, valour and romance. Provides great insight into the cultural origins of modern Arabs. These epic poems, still recited by professional storytellers in coffee-houses, particularly in Syria and Jordan, formed the basis for European medieval romances and chivalrous virtues.

The Arabian Desert: A Chronicle of Contrast, John Carter (Immel, 1983).

Arabian Essays, Ghazi Algosaibi (Kegan Paul International, 1982). Sensitive essays on a wide range of topics portraying the Arab point of view.

Aramco and Its World.

The Art of Arabian Costume, Heather Colyer Ross (Kegan Paul International, 1982).

Bedouin Jewellery in Saudi Arabia, Heather Colyer Ross (Stacey International, 1978).

Birth of Saudi Arabia: Britain and the Rape of the House of Sa'ud, Gary Troeller (Frank Cass, 1976).

A Doctor in Saudi Arabia, G.E. Moloney (Regency, 1985). (Personal Observations.)

Endings, Abd al-Rahman Munif (trans. Roger Allen) (Quartet, 1988). (Fiction.)

Everyday Life in the Harem, Babs Rule (W.H. Allen, 1986).

From Prince to King: Royal Succession in the House of Saud in the Twentieth Century (New York University Press, 1984).

Golden Days in the Desert, Betty Lipscombe Vincett (Immel, 1984). (Flowering plants.)

Ibn Saud, 'Abd al-'Aziz ihn 'Abd ar-Rahman, King of Saudi Arabia (Collins Harvill, 1986).

Inland Birds of Saudi Arabia, Jill Silsby (Immel, 1980).

Bedouins of Arabia, Thierry Mauger (Kegan Paul International, 1989).

Islam, the Straight Path, John L. Esposito (Oxford University Press, 1988). (A very readable, well-organised and thorough description of every aspect of the Islamic religion. Highly recommended.)

Leading Merchant Families of Saudi Arabia, John R.L. Carter (Scorpion Press, 1979).

The Makkah Massacre and Future of the Haramain, Zafar Bangash (Open Press, 1988).

Mineral Wealth of Saudi Arabia, Christopher Spencer (photos by Octave Farra) (Immel, 1987).

Modernity and Tradition: the Saudi Equation (Kegan Paul, 1990).

Public Land Distribution in Saudi Arabia, Hassan Hamza Hajrah (Longman in association with the Municipality of Jiddah and the University of Durham, Centre for Middle Eastern and Islamic Studies, 1983).

The Red Sea, Peter Vine (Immel, 1985).

Red Sea Safety: A Guide to Dangerous Marine Animals (Immel, 1987).

The Saudi Arabia Medical Guide (Immel, 1989).

Saudi Arabian Village in Transition: Study of a 'Bedouin Village', Motoko Katakura (University of Tokyo Press, 1977).

Saudi Arabia through the Eyes of an Artist, Malin Basil (Immel, 4th rev. edn 1977).

Saudi Cooking of Today, Ashkhain Skipwith (Stacey International, 1985).

The Saudis: Inside the Desert Kingdom, Sandra Mackey (Harrap, 1987).

Spirit of the Wind, Keith Collie (Immel, 1982). (Arab horses.)

A Thousand and One Coffee Mornings: Scenes from Saudi Arabia, Miranda Miller (Owen, 1989).

Understanding Arabs, A Guide for Westerners (Intercultural Press, 1987). This is an introduction to Arab personality, values, beliefs and social practices, written for non-specialists for the purpose of lessening cross-cultural misconceptions.

Wild Flowers of Central Saudi Arabia, Betty Lipscombe Vincett (E.W. Classey, 1977).

Women in Saudi Arabia: Ideology and Behaviour among the Elite (Columbia University Press, 1986).

'Women of Arabia', Marianne Alireza, *National Geographic*, October 1987. A fascinating account of Saudi women from all social classes and at all ages, with wonderful pictures.

Yamani: The Inside Story, Jeffrey Robinson (Simon & Schuster, 1988). (Sheikh Ahmed Zaki.)

BUSINESS/BANK/FINANCE/ECONOMIC

Business and Law in Saudi Arabia, G. Mutawakil (Immel., 1986).

Business Guide to Saudi Arabia (Longman World of Information Series) (Longman, 1984).

Business Laws of Saudi Arabia (Middle East Business Law Series), trans. Nicola H. Karam (Graham & Trotman, 1987).

Businessman's Guide to Saudi Arabia, Anthony Purdy (Arlington Books, 1976).

Business Opportunities in Saudi Arabia (Metra Consulting, 4th edn, 1985).

Economy of Saudi Arabia, Donald Moliver and Paul Abbondante (Praeger, 1980).

A Guide to the Saudi Arabian Economy, John R. Presley (Macmillan, 1984).

Industrial Development in Saudi Arabia: Opportunities for Joint Ventures, Caroline Montagu (Committee for Middle East Trade, 1985). (Report prepared for COMET.)

Joint Ventures in the Kingdom of Saudi Arabia, J. Walmsley (Graham & Trotman, 2nd edn 1985).

Maritime Regulations in the Kingdom of Saudi Arabia, Hussein M. El-Sayed (Graham & Trotman, 1987).

Meccan Trade and the Rise of Islam, Patricia Crone (Basil Blackwell, 1987).

The Middle East and North Africa 1988 (Europa Publications 1987). (Lists the constitution, government, judicial system, religion, press, trade and industrial companies for each country.)

Middle East Business Information Guide, Averill Harrison (compiler) (Middle East Economic Digest, 1986). (Organised by country and lists books and articles on all aspects of business.)

The New Oil Market: Saudi Arabia's Resurging Initiative, S.M. al-Sabah (Eastlords, 1986).

Oil and Diplomacy: The Evolution of American Foreign Policy in Saudi Arabia, 1933-45, Rex J. Casillas (Garland, 1987).

Political Economy of Saudi Arabia: 'House Built on Sand', Helen Lackner (Ithaca Press, 1978).

Saudi Arabia: Achievements and Prospects: A Report, John R. Presley (Committee for Middle East Trade, 1984). (Prepared by COMET.)

Saudi Arabia, A MEED Practical Guide (Middle East Economic Digest, 2nd edn 1983). (This is thorough and detailed, and is periodically updated. Check for the latest edition.)

Saudi Arabia and the Oil Boom: 'Oil and Labour in the Middle East', Peter Woodward (Praeger, 1988).

The Saudi Arabian Economy, Ali D. Johany, Michele Berne et al. (Croom Helm, 1986).

Saudi Arabian Industrial Investment: An Analysis of Government

Business Relationships, Abdulfattah Soufi Wahib and Richard T. Mayer (Quorum Books (US); Eurospan, 1991).

Saudi Arabia: The Making of a Financial Giant, Arthur N. Young (Longman, 1983). (Studies in Middle Eastern civilisations.)

Saudi Arabia 2000: A Strategy for Growth, Jean Paul Cleron (Croom Helm, 1977).

Saudi Business and Labor Law: Its Interpretation and Application, A. Lerrick and Q.J. Mian (Graham & Trotman, 2nd edn, 1986).

The Saudi Financial System: In the Context of Western and Islamic Finance, Adrian M. Abdeen and Dale N. Shook (John Wiley, 1984).

POLITICAL/SOCIAL/HISTORICAL

Bedouin, Wayne Eastep (Stacey International, 1985). (Chiefly colour illustrations.)

The Foreign Policy of Saudi Arabia: The Formative Years 1902–1918 (Harvard University Press, 1986).

The Historical Mosques of Saudi Arabia, Geoffrey R.D. King (Longman, 1986).

The House of Saud, David Holden and Richard Johns (Sidgwick and Jackson, 1981).

In the Footsteps of the Camel: A Portrait of the Bedouins of Eastern Saudi Arabia in Mid-Century, Eleanor Nicholson (Stacey International, 1983).

Jerusalem and Mecca: The Typology of the Holy City in the Near East (New York University studies in Near Eastern Civilization, No.11), Francis Edward Peters (New York University Press, 1986).

The Kingdom of Saudi Arabia, Sir Norman Anderson (Stacey International, 8th fully rev. edn, 1990).

Makkah (Mecca) a Hundred Years Ago, or, C. Snouk (Hurgronje's Remarkable Albums (1885), S. Snouk Hurgronje (Immel, 1986).

Riyadh, Anthony Guise (Stacey International, 1988). (Chiefly illustrations, some colour.)

Saudi Arabia: A Case Study for Development, Fouad al- Farsy (KPI, completely rev. and updated edn, 1986).

Saudi Arabia in the 1980s: Foreign Policy, Security and Oil, William B. Quandt (Brookings Institution, 1982).

Saudi Arabia in the Oil Era: Regime and Elites: Conflict and Collaboration, Mordechai Abir (Croom Helm, 1988).

Saudi Arabia Past and Present, Shirley Kay and Basil Malin (Quartet Books, 1979).

Saudi Arabia: The Ceaseless Quest for Security (Defence Policies of Government to 1982), Nadav Safran (Belknap Press of Harvard University Press, 1985).

Saudi Arabia: The Military Balance in the Gulf and the Trends in the Arab-Israeli Military Balance: 'Gulf and the Search for Strategic Stability', Anthony H. Cordesman (Mansell, 1984).

Saudi Arabia Today: An Introduction to the Richest Oil State, Peter Hobday (Macmillan, 1978).

The West and the Security of the Arab Gulf, Mazher A. Hameed (Croom Helm, 1986).

Western Security Interests in Saudi Arabia, Anthony H. Cordesman (Croom Helm, 1986).

TRAVEL

Arabian Sands, Wilfred Thesiger (Allen Lane, 1977). (A riveting account of the first crossing of the Rub' al Khali (the Empty Quarter) from south to north. This is an almost impossible route because of the lack of even the most brackish water.)

Berlitz Travel Guide to Saudi Arabia (Berlitz, 1987).

Colours of the Arab Fatherland, Angelo Pesce (comp.) (Oasis, 1975). (Description and travel, chiefly colour illustrations.)

The Empty Quarter, H. St. John Philby (Constable, 1986). (This book is a description of the great south desert of Arabia, telling of the author's explorations in the 1930s.)

Juggernaut: Trucking to Saudi Arabia, Robert Hutchinson (Heinemann, 1987).

Let's Visit Saudi Arabia, Martin Mulloy (Chelsea House, 1987).

A Pilgrimage to the Nejd, Lady Anne Blunt (Century Publishing, 1985).

We recommend that you request copies of a beautiful quarterly magazine, *Saudi Arabia*, published by the Royal Embassy of Saudi Arabia, 30 Belgrave Square, London SW1. The Embassy also publishes a monthly newsletter titled *Saudi Arabia*, as well as nine brochures: 'Facts and Figures', 'Islam', 'History', 'Education and Human Resources', 'Energy and Mineral Resources', 'Transportation and Communications', 'Agriculture and Water Resources', 'Health and Social Services' and 'Sports and Recreation'. All are available through the Information Office.

OTHER TITLES IN THIS SERIES

How to Get a Job Abroad, Roger Jones (How To Books, 2nd end, 1991).

How to Study Abroad, Teresa Tinsley (How To Books, 1990).

How to Teach Abroad, Roger Jones (How To Books, 1989).

Useful Addresses

EMBASSIES AND CONSULATES

In Saudi Arabia
British Embassy, PO Box 94351, Riyadh 11693. Tel: Riyadh (1)
488 0077.

HM Consulate General, PO Box 393, Jiddah 21411. Tel: (2) 691
5952/6864/7280/7440/8368/8704. Telex: 601043 BRITAIN SJ.
Fax: 691 7440.

In the United Kingdom
Royal Embassy of Saudi Arabia, 30 Belgrave Square, London
SW1. Tel: (071) 235 0831; (071) 245 9779; (071) 245 9787; (071)
245 9884.

Commercial Office, Royal Embassy of Saudi Arabia, 154 Bromp-
ton Road, London SW3. Tel: (071) 589 7246.

Consulate, Royal Embassy of Saudi Arabia, 30 Belgrave Square,
London SW1. Tel: (071) 235 0303; (071) 235 9038.

Health Office, Royal Embassy of Saudi Arabia, 119 Harley Street,
London W1. Tel: (071) 935 9931. Also: 22 Holland Park,
London W11. Tel: (071) 221 7575.

GOVERNMENT ORGANISATIONS AND AGENCIES

Saudi Arabia

Ministries
Ministry of Agriculture and Water, PO Box 2639, Riyadh 11461.

(Agricultural Affairs, Water Resource Development, Grain
Silos and Flour Mills Organisation: semi-autonomous)

Ministry of Commerce, Riyadh 11162. (Domestic and Foreign
Trade, Companies Registration, Joint Committee for Investigation of Commercial Disputes, Hotels, Chambers of Commerce and Industry)

Ministry of Communications, Riyadh 11178. (Roads and Bridges,
Transportation, Saudi Government Railroad Organisation–
Damman)

Ministry of Defence and Aviation, Riyadh 11165. (Armed Forces,
Presidency of Civil Aviation–Jiddah, Meteorology–Jiddah,
Military Ordnance Factories)

Ministry of Education, Riyadh 11148. (Elementary and Secondary
Education, Presidency of Girls' Education)

Ministry of Finance and National Economy, Riyadh 11177.
(Customs, Zakat and Income Tax, Budget, Budgetary Affairs,
State Properties, Statistics, National Computer Centre)

Ministry of Foreign Affairs, Riyadh 11124. (Political Affairs,
Institute of Diplomatic Studies)

Ministry of Health, PO Box 21217, Riyadh 11176. (Curative
Medicine, Preventive Medicine)

Ministry of Higher Education, PO Box 1683, Riyadh 11153.
(University Education)

Ministry of Industry and Electricity, PO Box 5729, Riyadh 11127.
(Electricity, Investment of Foreign Capital, Licensing of Manufacturing Enterprises)

Ministry of Information, PO Box 843, Riyadh 11161. (Radio and
Television, Press and Publications, Public Relations)

Ministry of the Interior, PO Box 3743, Riyadh 11439. (District
Governorates, Criminal Affairs, Public Security, Fire Brigades,
Passport and Nationality, Civil Defence, National Information
Centre, Public Morality Committee, Frontier Force, Special
Security Force, Traffic, Prisons, Police, Interpol)

Ministry of Labour and Social Affairs, Code No. 11157, Umar Bin
Khattab Street, Riyadh. (Social Security, Vocational Training,

General Organisation for Social Insurance—Riyadh, Presidency of Youth Welfare–semi-autonomous, Office of Affairs for the Blind, Civil Service, General Office for Social Insurance)

Ministry of Municipal and Rural Affairs, Riyadh 11136. (Town Planning, Sewerage and Water).

Ministry of Petroleum and Mineral Resources, Riyadh 11191. Petroleum, Mineral Resources–Jiddah)

Ministry of Pilgrimage (Hajj) and Endowments (Awqaf), Riyadh 11183. (Mosques, Religious Observances, Pilgrimage, Religious Research)

Ministry of Planning, PO Box 358, Riyadh 11182. (Development Plan, Royal Commission for Jubail and Yanbu)

Ministry of Posts Telegraphs and Telephones (PTT), Riyadh 11112. (Arab Satellite Communications Organisation)

Ministry of Public Works and Housing, Riyadh 11151. (Public Housing Programme, Facilities for Pilgrimage)

Chambers of Commerce and Industry
Council of Saudi Chambers of Commerce and Industry, PO Box 16683, Riyadh. Location: Riyadh Chamber of Commerce and Industry Building, Dhabbab Street. Tel: (1) 404 0044; (1) 405 4277. Telex: 401054 TJARYH SJ.

There are active Chambers of Commerce and Industry at the following addresses:

PO Box 722, Abha. Location: Ringroad, behind Asir traffic police. Tel: (7) 244 9488/9480). Telex: 901125/6 SOUTH SJ

PO Box 440, Ar-Ar. Tel: (4) 622 6544. Telex: 612058 TJARYH SJ.

PO Box 311, Al Baha. Tel: (7) 725 4116/0476. Telex: 431048 CHRCBH SJ.

PO Box 719, Dammam. Location: Chamber Building, Post Office Road. Tel: (3) 833 8660. Telex: 801086 CHAMBER SJ.

PO Box 1291, Hail. Tel: (6) 532 4494/9349. Telex: 811086 SHAMAL SJ.

PO Box 1519, Hofuf, Al Hasa. Location: Dammam Road. Tel: (3) 582 0458. Telex: 861140 HASACO SJ.

PO Box 1264, Jiddah. Location: Chamber of Commerce and Industry Building, Mina-Qasr Road, near Television Road. Tel: (2) 647 1100/7169. Telex: 601069 GHURFA SJ.

PO Box 201, Jizan. Location: Ministry of Commerce Building off Main Square. Tel: (7) 317 1519.

PO Box 165, Majm'a. Tel: (6) 432 0268. Telex: 247020 GHURFA SJ.

PO Box 1086, Mecca. Location: Al Gazzah Street. Tel: (2) 574 4202/5775. Telex: 540011 CHAMEC SJ.

PO Box 443, Medina. Location: Bab al Shami. Tel: (4) 822 5190/5380. Telex: 470009 ICCMD SJ.

PO Box 444, Buraidah (Qassim). Location: Al Wahedah Street, (Al Mara Street end). Tel: (6) 324 2887/323 6104. Telex: 801060 SINAIA SJ.

PO Box 596, Riyadh. Location: Riyadh Chamber of Commerce and Industry Building, Dhabbab Street. Tel: (1) 404 0300/3373/ 0044. Telex: 401054 TJARYH SJ.

PO BOX 567, Tabuk. Location: Bahglaf Building, Main Street (behind Saudi Office). Tel: (4) 422 0464/2736.

PO Box 1005, Taif. Location: Airport Road, opposite Technical High School. Tel: (2) 736 4626. Telex: 751009 GHURFA SJ.

PO Box 58, Yanbu. Location: King Adbul Aziz Street. Tel: (4) 322 4257/8. Telex: 661036 GHURFA SJ.

British Commercial Representative
British Trade Office, PO Box 88, Dhahran Airport 31421. Tel: (3) 857 0595. Telex: 870028 WATEKA SJ. Fax: (3) 857 8130.

British Council Offices
(Main Office), PO Box 2701, Riyadh 11461. Tel: (1) 402 1650; (1) 404 3193/2795. Location: off Washem Street, Murabba.

PO Box 3424, Jiddah 21471. Tel: (2) 667 2867. Telex: 403962 BRCOUN SJ. Location: Villa 14(10) in residential development on al Fadhl Street, Hamra.

United Kingdom
Arab–British Chamber of Commerce, 6 Belgrave Square, London SW1X 8PH. Tel: (071) 235 4369. Telex: 299484 ARABISG.

BBC External Services, Export Liaison Unit, Bush House, Strand, London WC2B 4PH. Tel: (071) 257 2039. Telex: 265781 a/b BBC HQ G for attention of EXPORT LIAISON BUSH. Also: BBC External Services Producer at any of the BBC Regional Offices.

Birmingham Chamber of Commerce and Industry, 75 Harbourne Road, Birmingham B15 3DH. Tel: (021) 454 6171.

Central Office of Information, Head Office, Hercules House, Westminster Bridge Road, London SE1 7DU. Tel: (071) 928 2345. Telex: 915444 a/b COILDN G. Also Regional Offices.

Confederation of British Industry, Centre Point, 103 New Oxford Street, London WC1A 1DU. Tel: (071) 379 7400.

Export Credits Guarantee Department, Head Office, PO Box 272, Export House, 50 Ludgate Hill, London EC4M 7AY. Tel: (071) 382 7000. Telex: 883601 a/b ECGDHQ (A–C) LDN.

London Chamber of Commerce and Industry, Middle East and North Africa Section, 69–73 Cannon Street, London EC4N 5AB. Tel: (071) 248 4444.

Manchester Chamber of Commerce, 56 Oxford Street, Manchester M60 7HJ. Tel: (061) 263 3210.

The Middle East Association, Bury House, 33 Bury Street, St James's, London SW 1 6AX. Tel: (071) 839 2137/8/9.

Saudi Arabian Information Centre, Cavendish House, 18 Cavendish Square, London W1. Tel: (071) 629 8803.

Department of Trade and Industry, 1–19 Victoria Street, London SW1H 0ET. Tel: (071) 215 5000.

DTI Regional Offices
DTI South East London Office (covering Greater London),

Bridge Place, 88–89 Eccleston Square, London SW1V 1PT. Tel: (071) 215 0575. Telex: 297124 SEREX G. Fax: (071) 828 1105.

Area Office Cambridge (covering Bedfordshire, Cambridgeshire, Essex, Hertfordshire, Norfolk and Suffolk), Building A, Westbrook Research Centre, Milton Road, Cambridge CB4 1YG. Tel: (0223) 461939. Telex: 81582 DTI EAO. Fax: (0223) 461941.

Area Office Reading (covering Berkshire, Buckinghamshire, Hampshire, Isle of Wight and Oxfordshire), 40 Caversham Road, Reading, Berkshire RG1 7EB. Tel: (0734) 395600. Telex: 847799 DTI RDG. Fax: (0734) 502818.

Area Office Reigate (covering Kent, Surrey, East Sussex and West Sussex), Douglas House, London Road, Reigate, Surrey RH2 9QP. Tel: (0737) 226900. Telex: 918364 DTI RGT G. Fax: (0737) 223491.

DTI North East, Stanegate House, 2 Groat Market, Newcastle-upon-Tyne NE1 1YN. Tel: (091) 232 4722. Telex: 53178 DTI TYN G. Fax: (091) 232 6742.

DTI North West, Sunley Tower, Piccadilly Plaza, Manchester M1 4BA. Tel: (061) 236 2171. Telex: 667104 DTI MCHR. Fax: (061) 228 3740.

DTI Yorkshire and Humberside, Priestley House, Park Row, Leeds LS1 5LF. Tel: (0532) 44371. Telex: 557925 DTI LDS G. Fax: (0532) 421038.

DTI South West, The Pithay, Bristol BS1 2PB. Tel: (0272) 272666. Telex: 44214 DTI BTL G. Fax: (0272) 299494.

DTI West Midlands, Ladywood House, Stephenson Street, Birmingham B2 4DT. Tel: (021) 631 6181. Telex: 337919 DTI BHAM G. Fax: (021) 643 5500.

DTI East Midlands, Severns House, 20 Middle Pavement, Nottingham NG1 7DW. Tel: (0602) 506181. Telex: 37143 DTI NOT G. Fax: (0602) 587074.

The following also act as Department of Trade and Industry regional Offices:

Northern Ireland: Industrial Development Board for Northern Ireland, IDB House, 64 Chichester Street, Belfast BT1 4JX. Tel: (0232) 233233. Telex: 747025 IDB NI G.

Scottish Export Office: Industry Department for Scotland, Alhambra House, 45 Waterloo Street, Glasgow G2 6AT. Tel: (041) 248 2855. Telex: 777883 IDS GW.

Welsh Office Industry Department: New Crown Building, Cathays Park, Cardiff CF1 3NQ. Tel: (0222) 825097. Telex: 498228 WOCARD G.

Other organisations associated with the DTI
Committee for Middle East Trade (COMET), 33 Bury Street, St James's, London SW1Y 6AX. Tel: (071) 839 1170.

Export Intelligence Service: contact the local Regional Office of the Department of Trade and Industry.

Fairs and Promotions Branch, Department of Trade and Industry, Dean Bradley House, 52 Horseferry Road, London SW1P 2AG. Tel: (071) 276 2493.

Simplification of International Trade Procedures Board (SITPRO), Almack House, 26–28 King Street, London SW1Y 6QW. Tel: (071) 930 0532. Telex: 919130 SITPRO G.

Groups in Parliament
Labour Middle East Council, 21 Collingham Road, London SW5 0NU. Tel: (071) 373 8414.

Conservative Middle East Council, c/o House of Commons, Whitehall, London SW1.

Liberal Middle East Council, 12 Henrietta Street, Covent Garden, London WC2. Tel: (071) 379 7973.

British–Saudi Arabian Group, c/o House of Commons, Whitehall, London SW1.

Parliamentary Association for Euro-Arab Co-operation, c/o House of Commons, Whitehall, London SW1.

EDUCATIONAL/CULTURAL ORGANISATIONS

Arab Cultural Trust, 13a Hillgate Street, London W8. Tel: (071) 727 3131.

Arab & Iranian Centre, 66 Strand, London WC2. Tel: (071) 839 2651.

Arab & Iranian Studies, 66 Strand, London WC2. Tel: (071) 839 1766.

Arab—British Centre Ltd, 21 Collingham Road, London SW5 0NU. Tel: (071) 373 8414.

Arabic Centre, 51/53 Edgware Road, London W2. Tel: (071) 402 7913.

Arab Women's Council, 8 Redcliffe Gardens, London SW10. Tel: (071) 373 0688.

Council for the Advancement of Arab–British Understanding (CAABU), 21 Collingham Road, London SW5 0NU. Tel: (071) 373 8414.

Gulf Centre for Strategic Studies Ltd, Charterhouse Buildings, London EC1. Tel: (071) 253 3805.

Muslim Women's Association, 146 Park Road, London NW8. Tel: (081) 946 1052.

Saudi Arabian Cultural Office, 29 Belgrave Square, London SW1. Tel: (071) 245 9944; (071) 235 8334.

Saudi Arabian Educational Office, 29 Belgrave Square, London SW1. Tel: (071) 245 6481.

Saudi-British Society, 21 Collingham Road, London SW5 0NU. Tel: (071) 373 8414.

Centres for Arabic/Islamic Studies at UK Universities

Department of Geography, University of ABERDEEN, St Mary's High Street, Old Aberdeen. Tel: (0224) 4024.

Faculty of Oriental Studies, University of CAMBRIDGE, Sidgwick Avenue, Cambridge.

School of Oriental Studies, Elvet Hill, DURHAM DH1 3TH. Tel: (0385) 64971, Ext. 701.

Department of Islamic and Middle Eastern Studies, University of EDINBURGH, 7 Buccleuch Place, Edinburgh EH8 9LW. Tel: (031) 667 1011, ext. 6390.

The Centre of Arab Gulf Studies, University of EXETER, Thornlea, New North Road, Exeter, Devon. Tel: (0392) 77911.

Department of Arabic and Islamic Studies, Thornlea, New North Road, EXETER, Devon. Tel: (0392) 77911.

Department of Arabic, University of GLASGOW, Glasgow. Tel: (041) 339 8855.

Department of Sociology and Social Anthropology, University of HULL, York. Tel: (0482) 46311.

Institute of Islamic Studies, University of LANCASTER, Bailrigg, Lancaster. Tel: (0524) 65201.

Department of Semitic Studies, University of LEEDS, Leeds LS2 9JT. Tel: (0532) 431751.

School of Oriental and African Studies, University of LONDON, Malet Street, London WC2. Tel: (071) 637 2388.

LONDON School of Economics and Political Science, Houghton Street, London WC2A 2AE. Tel: (071) 405 7686.

Department of Social Anthropology, University of MANCHESTER, Dover Street, Mancheser. Tel: (061) 273 7121.

Department of Religious Studies, University of NEWCASTLE-UPON-TYNE, Armstrong Building, Newcastle-upon-Tyne NE1 7RU. Tel: (0632) 328511.

Faculty of Oriental Studies, University of OXFORD, Pusey Lane, Oxford OX1 2LE. Tel: Oxford (0865) 278200.

Middle East Centre, St Antony's College, OXFORD. Tel: Oxford (0865) 59651.

Department of Arabic Studies, University of ST ANDREWS, St Andrews, Fife. Tel: (0334) 76161.

Department of International Politics, University College of WALES, Aberystwyth, Dyfed. Tel: (0970) 3111.

Centre for Islamic Studies, St David's University College,

University of WALES, Lampeter, Dyfed SA48 7ED. Tel: Lampeter (0570) 422351. Director: Mr M. Mashuq ibn Ally.

TRANSLATING SERVICES

Arabic Advertising & Publishing Co. Ltd, Translators & Interpreters, Berkeley Square House, Berkeley Square, London W1. Tel: (071) 409 0953.

Arabic Commercial & Technical Translations, Marzell House, 116 North End Road, London W14. Tel: (071) 381 0967.

Arabic Language Services (UK) Ltd, 20 Colet Gardens, London W14. Tel: (081) 748 3896.

Arabic Linguistic Services Ltd, Translation Office, 459 Finchley Road, London NW3. Tel: (071) 431 1815.

Arabic Technical Translation Co., Translators, Interpreters, Printers, 76 Shoe Lane, London EC4. Tel: (071) 583 8690; (071) 353 5813.

Arabic Technical Translation & Print, Alpha House, 74 Maida Vale, London W9. Tel: (071) 624 2525.

Arabic Technical Translators, 11 Uxbridge Road, London W12. (081) 749 3211.

Arabic Translations, 64 Queen Street, London EC4. Tel: (071) 248 8707.

Arabic Translations & Typesetting, Berkeley Square House, Berkeley Square, London W1. (071) 409 0953.

Arabic/English Typesetters Ltd, Translators/Interpreters, 34 Percy Street, London W1. Tel: (071) 636 2911.

Interlingua TTI Ltd. Translation, Typesetting, Interpreting, Imperial House, Kingsway London WC2. Tel: (071) 240 5361.

TRAVEL SERVICES/AIRLINES

AA Business Travel, FREEPOST, Fanum House, Basingstoke, Hants RG21 2EA. Tel: Basingstoke (0256) 492632.

Arab Tours Ltd, 78 Marylebone Lane, London W1. Tel: (071) 935 3273.

Gulf Air, 10 Albemarle Street, London W1. Tel: (Administration) (071) 409 0191; (Reservations) (071) 408 1717.

Gulf Travel, 25 Henriques Street, London E1. Tel: (071) 481 3166.

Middle East Airlines SAL, Sales & Administration, 48 Park Street, London W1. Tel: (071) 493 5681. Administration, Sales & Accountants, Tel: (071) 493 6321.

Middle East Air Services Ltd, 48 Park Street, London W1. Tel: (071) 491 2974; (071) 629 7761.

Middle East Travel Centre Ltd, Travel Agent, 252 Linen Hall, Regent Street, London W1. Tel: (071) 439 1544.

Saudi Tourist & Travel Bureau, 36 St James's Street, London SW1. Tel: (071) 491 2907.

SAUDIA—Saudi Arabian Airlines, 171 Regent Street, London W1. Tel: (Reservations) (081) 995 7777; (Car) London Radiophone 216077. Also: 508 Chiswick High Road, London W4. (Administration, District Office, Sales, Finance Departments) Tel: (081) 995 7755. Also: Tel: Manchester (061) 833 9575.

BANKS

Arab African International Bank, Salisbury House, Finsbury Circus, London EC2. Tel: (071) 628 8481; (071) 638 0931; Dealers (071) 628 9571. Also: 11 Carlos Place, London W1. Tel: (071) 408 0323.

Arab Bankers Association, 1 Hanover Street, London W1. Tel: (071) 629 5423. Arab Banking Corporation, 1 Moorgate, London EC2. London Branch, Tel: (071) 726 4599; Investment Banking Division, Tel: (071) 628 9841; ABC (London) Services Ltd, Tel: (071) 726 4108; Representative's Office, Tel: (071) 606 5461.

Arab Bank Ltd, Empire House, St Martins-le-Grand, London EC1. London Radiophone (car): 216262. Also: 118 Kensington High Street, London W8. Tel: (071) 376 1158; (071) 937 3547. 13 Moorgate, London EC2. Tel: (071) 315 8500; (071) 606 2463. 114 Park Lane, London W1. Tel: (071) 408 1505; (071) 629 5906.

Arab National Bank, 40 Piccadilly, London W1. Tel: (071) 287 2335.

Gulf Bank KSC, 1 College Hill, London EC4. Tel: (071) 408 1717.

Gulf Guarantee Bank PLC, 139 Park Lane, London W1. Tel: (071) 493 1969.

Gulf International Bank, 2 Cannon Street, London EC4. Tel: (071) 248 6411.

Middle East Bank Ltd, 1 Lombard Street, London EC3. Tel: (071) 283 2201.

Saudi American Bank, Nightingale House, 65 Curzon Street, London W1. Tel: (071) 355 4411.

Saudi British Bank, Representative's Office, 4 Stanhope Gate, London W1. Tel: (071) 409 2567.

Saudi International Bank, 99 Bishopsgate, London EC2. Tel: (071) 638 2323.

PUBLISHERS

Arab Encyclopaedia House, 2 Greville Lodge, Westbourne Grove Terrace, London W2. Tel: (071) 229 4045; (071) 229 3880.

Arab International Media Centre, Publishing and Printing, 375 Leatherhead Road, Kingston, Surrey. Tel: (071) 434 4141.

Arabic Advertising & Publishing Co. Ltd, Translators & Interpreters, Berkeley Square House, Berkeley Square, London W1. Tel: (071) 409 0953.

British Business (Department of Trade & Industry Magazine). Tel: (071) 215 3935/6/7.

Middle East Agribusiness Journal, Queensway House, 2 Queensway, Redhill, Surrey. Tel: Redhill (0737) 768611.

Middle East Annual Review, Publishers. Saffron Walden 21150.

Middle East Computing Magazine, Quadrant House, The Quadrant, Sutton, Surrey. Tel: (Editorial) (081) 661 8760.

Middle East Economic Digest Ltd, 21 John Street, London WC1N 2BP. Tel: (071) 404 5513.

Middle East Electricity Magazine, Quadrant House, The Quadrant, Sutton, Surrey. Tel: (Editorial) (081) 661 8742.

Middle East Health Magazine, Quadrant House, The Quadrant, Sutton, Surrey. Tel: (Editorial) (081) 661 8721.

Middle East News Agency, Communications House, Gough Square, London EC4. Tel: (071) 353 5455.

Middle East Publications Ltd, Newspapers Distributors, 10 Barley Mow Passage, London W4. Tel: (081) 994 6477. Also: 188 Sutton Court Road, London W4. Tel: (081) 994 0515.

Middle East Travel Magazine, 69 Great Queen Street, London WC2. Tel: (071) 404 4333.

Middle East Water & Sewage Journal, Queensway House, 2 Queensway, Redhill, Surrey. Tel: Redhill (0737) 768611.

Saudi Press Agency, 18 Cavendish Square, London W1. Tel: (071) 495 0418; (071) 495 0419.

GENERAL BUSINESS/COMMERCE

Anderson Gardiner (Shipping) Ltd, Dept AGS, Orwell House, Ferry Lane, Felixstowe, Suffolk IP11 8QL. Tel: (0394) 673964. Telex: 987771/987159. Fax: (0394) 674454. Cables: Anders Felixstowe.

Arab Business Communication, 15 Hollingbourne Gardens, London W13. Tel: (081) 997 7218.

Arab Halal Meat Centre Ltd, 185 Queensway, London W2. Tel: (071) 229 2655.

Arab Insurance Group, Insurance Underwriters, Plantation House, Fenchurch Street, London EC3. Tel: (071) 626 4155.

Arab International Gas & Transportation Ltd, 34 Savile Row, London W1. Tel: (071) 434 2431.

Arab International Trust Co. Ltd, 6 Cork Street, London W1. Tel: (071) 434 4141; (071) 734 5514.

Arab Post UK Ltd, 633 Linen Hall, 162 Regent Street, London W1. Tel: (071) 734 6918.

Arabco-Goldsecure Ltd, Trading Company, 1 Hyde Park Place, London W2. Tel: (071) 723 3568.

Arabconsult Business Service Inc., 49 Park Lane, London W1. (071) 491 2822.

Arabian Careers Ltd, 115 Shaftesbury Avenue, London WC2. Tel: (071) 379 7877.

Arabian Computers Ltd, 15 Uxbridge Street, London W8, Tel: (071) 221 9269.

Arabian Establishment for Trade & Shipping, 36 St James's Street, London W1. Tel: (071) 491 2907.

Arabian Industrialists Ltd, 12 Bank Place, London W2. Tel: (071) 229 2051.

Arabian Oil Co. Ltd, London Representative's Office, 61 Brook Street, London W1. Tel: (071) 499 6438. Also: London Branch of Field Office, same address. Tel: (071) 499 3238.

Arabian Video Time Ltd, Advertising Contractors, Irving House, Irving Street, London WC2. Tel: (071) 839 4231.

Arabic Graphic, 134 Curtain Road, London EC2. Tel: (071) 739 8000.

The Association of Manufacturers of Domestic Electrical Appliances (AMDEA), Leicester House, 8 Leicester Street, London WC2H 7BN. Tel: (071) 437 0678; Telex: 263536; Fax: (071) 494 1094. Senior Technical Officer: S.A. MacConnacher.

K.W. Franks Shipping Ltd, 47 North Street, Sudbury, Suffolk CO10 0BT. Tel: Sudbury (0787) 312153. Telex: 987549 PRANKS G. Fax: Sudbury (0787) 79588.

K.W. Franks Shipping (Ireland) Ltd, 19 Fitzwilliam Square, Dublin 2, Republic of Ireland. Tel: Dublin (010 3531) 611956/7. Telex: 91587 FRKS EI. Fax: Dublin (010 3531) 611956, Ext. 25.

Gulf Consumer Goods Co. Ltd, Import, Export, Wholesale Warehouse, Gulf House, Stephenson Street, London E16, Tel: (071) 474 0177; (071) 474 3702; (071) 511 2613.

Gulf Development Co. Ltd, Gulf House, Park Lane, London W1. Tel: (071) 629 6363.

Gulf Freight Forwarding Ltd, 22 Ariel Way, Wood Lane, London W12. Tel: (081) 749 7832.

Gulf International (UK) Ltd, Export, Import, 46 Mount Street, London W1. (071) 499 9948; (071) 493 2688.

Gulf Investments Advisory Service, 7a Malvern Mews, London NW6. Tel: (071) 328 5642.

Gulf Medical Consultants Ltd, 24 Welbeck Street, London W1. Tel: (071) 486 3026; (071) 224 4216.

Gulf Oil (Great Britain) Ltd, Importers, Distributors, 288 Borough High Street, London SE1. Tel: (071) 403 0754. Also Minoco Wharf, London E16. Tel: (071) 476 3131. Also: 77 Mortlake High Street, London SW14. Tel: (081) 878 7531.

Gulf Pearl Ltd, 77 Westbourne Grove, London W2. Tel: (071) 229 8124. Also: 68 Westbourne Grove, London W2. Tel: (071) 792 3692.

Gulf Properties & Investments, 40 Great Portland Street, London W1. Tel: (071) 637 4782.

Gulf Resources, 148 Old Park Lane, London W1. Tel: (071) 409 0435.

Gulf Shipping Lines Ltd, 60 Bunhill Row, London EC1. Tel: (071) 251 1600.

Gulf Trading Co. Ltd, 153 Earl's Court Road, London SW5. Tel: (071) 244 6699; (071) 244 6834.

Gulf Transac Ltd, Exporters, Greenfield House, 69 Manor Road, Wallington, Surrey. Tel: (081) 669 8237.

Gulf & UK Industrial Consultants Ltd, 29 Kensington Square, London W8. Tel: (071) 937 0855; (071) 937 1486; (Car) London Radiophone 216948.

Gulf & Western Group Ltd, West Garden Place, London W2. Tel: (071) 402 8291.

The Institution of Electrical Engineers, Savoy Place, London WC2R 0BL. Tel: (071) 240 1871; Telex: 261176 IEELDN-G;

Fax: Council Officer (071) 379 7707; Learned Society and Conferences (071) 497 3633; Library (071) 497 3557; Qualifications (071) 497 3609; Technical Affairs (071) 497 2143; General (071) 240 7735. Secretary: Dr J.C. Williams, PhD, CEng, FIEE; Director, Technical Affairs: J.P. Cutting.

Saudi Arabian Representative: Dr Mohamed N. Khayata, BSc (Eng), PhD, FIEE, c/o Saudi Fund for Development, PO Box 50483, Riyadh, Saudi Arabia. Tel: (1) 464 0292 (Office); (1) 488 2760 (Home).

Middle East Air Services Ltd, 48 Park Street, London W1. Tel: (071) 491 2974; (071) 629 7761.

Middle East Associates, Finance Consultants, 5 Cromwell Place, London SW7. Tel: (071) 581 5711.

The Middle East Association, 33 Bury Street, London SW1. Tel: (071) 839 2137.

Middle East Cargo Services, Import/Export agents, 60 Lillie Road, London SW6. Tel: (071) 937 0881; (071) 937 1148.

Middle East Consultants, Marketing Consultants, Unit 13, The Glassmill, 1 Battersea Bridge Road, London SW11. Tel: (071) 924 2980.

Middle East Development Co., 11 Aberdeen Court, Aberdeen Park, London N5. Tel: (071) 354 1564.

Middle East Services Ltd, 9 Connaught Street, London W2. Tel: (071) 724 2424.

Middle East Trade & Exhibitions Ltd, 2 Welbeck House, Welbeck Street, London W1. Tel: (071) 486 3741.

Middle East Wire & Wireless Ltd, Direct Communication Equipment, Unit 2, 106 Garratt Lane, London SW18. Tel: (081) 785 6422.

MK Electric Limited, Shrubbery Road, Edmonton, London N9 0PB. Tel: (081) 803 3355; International Sales Telex: 299464 MKINT G.

Saudi Investment Group Management Advisory Services (SIGMA), 36 St James's Street, London SW1. Tel: (071) 491 2907.

Saudi Research Marketing UK Ltd, 182 High Holborn, London
WC1. Tel: (071) 831 8181.

Saudia Charter Medical Ltd, 61 Harley Street, London W1. Tel:
(071) 323 9661.

Saudia Medical Ltd, 61 Harley Street, London W1. Tel: (071) 636
8395.

Technical Help to Exporters, BSI, Linford Wood, Milton Keynes,
MK14 6LE. Tel: Milton Keynes (0908) 220022.

LEGAL CONTACTS

Saudi Arabia
S.H. Amin, LlB, LlM, PhD, Director, Centre for Comparative
and International Law at Glasgow College. Author of Middle
East Legal Systems (1985). 10 Crown Road North, Glasgow
G12 9DH. Tel: (041) 339 1867. Telex: 779341 GCT-G. Fax:
(041) 331 1075.

The Law Firm of Salah Al-Hejailan, PO Box 1454, Riyadh 11431,
Saudi Arabia. Tel: (1) 479 2200. Telex: 400486. Fax: (1) 497
1717. Also: PO Box 15141, Jiddah 21444, Saudi Arabia. Tel:
(2) 653 4422. Telex: 606766. Fax: (2) 651 7241. Associated Firm
of Clifford Chance Amsterdam, Bahrain, Brussels, Hong Kong,
Madrid, New York, Paris, Singapore, Tokyo, United Arab
Emirates.

Gulf
Gulf Legal Services, Grosvenor Gardens House, Gorsvenor Gardens, London SW1. Tel: (071) 828 8265.

Counsel Practising in London
Jamal Nasir, PhD (London), Barrister-at-Law, 2 Stone Buildings,
Lincoln's Inn, London WC2A 3XB. Tel: (071) 405 3818.

Anis Al-Qasem, LLB, LLM, PhD (London). Diploma in Oil and
Gas Laws (Southern Methodist University, Dallas, Texas). L.
Jan. 1950. Libyan Bar. 2 Paper Buildings, Temple, London
EC4Y 7ET. Tel: (071) 353 9119/9110/0826. Telex: 885368
Temple G. Fax: (071) 583 3423.

W.M. Ballantyne, MA (Cantab.), Barrister-at-Law, 1 Hare Court, Temple, London EC4. Tel: (071) 353 3171. Telex: 8814 348 SINDEN. Fax: (071) 583 9127.

Riyadh

Baker & McKenzie, PO BOx 4288, Riyadh 11491, Saudi Arabia. Tel: (10966-1) 403 5566. Telex: 406034 ABOGAD SJ. Fax: (10966-1) 403 4794. Associated office of Baker & McKenzie, Aldwych House, Aldwych, London WC2B 4JP. Tel: (071) 242 6531. Telex: 25660. Fax: (071) 831 8611.

MISCELLANEOUS

Arab Line Ltd, 50 Maple Street, London W1. Tel: (071) 436 1375. Arab Research Centre, 5 Belgrave Square, London SW1. Tel: (071) 235 7642.

Arab Spacescene Corporation, The Glassmill, 1 Battersea Park Road, London SW11. Tel: (071) 223 3911; (071) 223 8641.

Middle East Executive Ltd, 7 Broadstone Place, London W1. Tel: (071) 935 3899.

Middle East Express Ltd, 188 Sutton Court Road, London W4. Tel: (081) 742 1859.

Index

How to Live & Work in Australia
Laura Veltman *Second edition*

The *Sydney-Sun-Herald* recently reported a massive 1,400 telephone calls a day to Australia House in London from would-be immigrants from Britain, with queues of personal callers stretching round the block. Never has there been such competition to get in. If you are competing for a place, you need **How to Live & Work in Australia**, packed from cover to cover with vital current information on costs, the crucial 'points' system, job opportunities, essential addresses, and domestic living in Australia today. 'One marvellous little book . . . has just been published . . . Called **How to Live & Work in Australia** it's written by Australian journalist Laura Veltman and she should know what she's talking about as she specialises in Australian migrant affairs. Written in a clear and entertaining style it provides all sorts of information (and) there's great good humour as Laura takes an honest look at Australian attitudes.' *Resident Abroad magazine* 'Of interest to young travellers, too.' *The Times* 'Over a million people apply to enter Australia every year—and last year only 140,000 were successful. This year the numbers are being cut even more to 125,000 . . . There has never been a better time to get hold of **How to Live & Work in Australia**.' *Southern X.*
224pp illustrated paperback. 0 7463 0583 4

How to Get a Job Abroad
Roger Jones BA(Hons) DipEd DPA
Second Edition

This popular title is essential reading for everyone planning to spend a period abroad. A key feature is the lengthy reference section of medium and long-term job opportunities and possibilities, arranged by region and country of the world, and by profession/occupation. There are more than 130 pages of specific contracts and leads, giving literally hundreds of addresses and much hard-to-find information. There is a classified guide to overseas recruitment agencies, and even a multi-lingual guide to writing application letters. 'A fine book for anyone considering even a temporary overseas job.' *The Evening Star.* 'A highly informative and well researched book . . . containing lots of hard information and a first class reference section . . . A superb buy.' *The Escape Committee Newsletter.* Roger Jones BA AKC DipTESL DipEd MInstAM DPA MBIM has himself worked abroad for many years and is a specialist writer on expatriate and employment matters.
288pp illus. 1 85703 003 6. 2nd edition